D0805121

Time Traveller's Handbook

929.1
D

C.J

Time Traveller's Handbook

A Guide to the Past

Althea Douglas

Ontario Genealogical Society

DUNDURN PRESS
TORONTO

DISCARD
STAUNTON PUBLIC LIBRARY

Copyright © Althea Douglas, 2011

All rights reserved. No part of this publication may be reproduced, stored in a retrieval system, or transmitted in any form or by any means, electronic, mechanical, photocopying, recording, or otherwise (except for brief passages for purposes of review) without the prior permission of Dundurn Press. Permission to photocopy should be requested from Access Copyright.

Editor: Ruth Chernia
Copy Editor: Nicole Chaplin
Design: Jesse Hooper
Printer: Webcom

Library and Archives Canada Cataloguing in Publication

Douglas, Althea, 1926-
Time traveller's handbook : what every family historian
needs to know / by Althea Douglas.

Co-published by Ontario Genealogical Society.
Includes bibliographical references and index.
Issued also in electronic format.
ISBN 978-1-55488-784-2

1. Genealogy. 2. History--Miscellanea. I. Ontario
Genealogical Society II. Title.

CS9.D69 2011   929'.1072   C2010-902708-6

1   2   3   4   5   15   14   13   12   11

We acknowledge the support of the **Canada Council for the Arts** and the **Ontario Arts Council** for our publishing program. We also acknowledge the financial support of the **Government of Canada** through the **Canada Book Fund** and **Livres Canada Books**, and the **Government of Ontario** through the **Ontario Book Publishers Tax Credit** program, and the **Ontario Media Development Corporation**.

Care has been taken to trace the ownership of copyright material used in this book. The author and the publisher welcome any information enabling them to rectify any references or credits in subsequent editions.

J. Kirk Howard, President

All images from the author's collection, unless otherwise indicated.

Printed and bound in Canada.
www.dundurn.com

Ontario Genealogical Society
Suite 102, 40 Orchard View Boulevard
Toronto, Ontario, Canada M4R 1B9
tel. (416) 489-0734   fax. (416) 489-9803
provoffice@ogs.on.ca   www.ogs.on.ca

Dundurn Press	Gazelle Book Services Limited	Dundurn Press
3 Church Street, Suite 500	White Cross Mills	2250 Military Road
Toronto, Ontario, Canada	High Town, Lancaster, England	Tonawanda, NY
M5E 1M2	LA1 4XS	U.S.A. 14150

Contents

Introduction

The past is a foreign country,
they do things differently there.
    — L.P. Hartley, *The Go-Between*

With such constant change, even the recent past can seem alien. The metric system has largely replaced the imperial measurement system I knew as a child. The shilling and the franc are gone, just like the thaler before them. Latin abbreviations are used less often and are frequently misunderstood; I sometimes have to pause with Roman numerals. As for those dates we had to memorize in history class, 1492 is probably one of the few remembered because of the rhyme: "Columbus sailed the ocean blue." Do you know how long it could take to cross the Atlantic by sail? Was the trip faster going from east to west or from west to east? Imagine sailing to India, a five-month trip around the Cape of Good Hope. No wonder late Victorians valued the steamship and Suez Canal.

And speaking of travel, what is the average speed of a man on horseback or in a coach and four? How far can those four horses pull a coach before they have to stop for a bait. What is a bait, anyhow? If the recent spate of films based loosely on Jane Austen's writings sent you back to reread her novels, you may know a few of the answers. Are you certain how titles are used, or just what they signify? Did you notice "Sir Reginald and Lady Norah," said to be the parents of Miss Amanda Price in *Lost in Austen*? That "Lady Norah" implies that even if her father was a rich fishmonger who had been knighted, her mother was at the very least the daughter of an Earl.

This sort of information is available on the Internet — somewhere — and you can waste a lot of time hunting for it. This guide is an attempt to bring together a lot of facts our ancestors once knew, took for granted, and used regularly. It also includes several lists of useful dates, as well as some words and expressions we have forgotten or whose meanings have changed, and a few abbreviations derived from the Latin that every schoolchild once studied.

Because many readers of this book will be family historians and researchers, an early chapter will consider documents and how to look at papers and artifacts that have survived from the past, as well as family legends and "mythinformation" that have been handed down over generations.

There are other holdovers from the past, customs and traditions we now consider undemocratic, quaint, or dismiss as a waste of time. Some of these derive from our colonial past. The provinces and territories that make up Canada were once a part of the French colonial empire, then of the British. Many of our government and civil institutions are rooted in either British or French ways of doing things, which these former imperial powers spread around the globe, just as they spread the use of their languages. Today, Canadians come from all over the world. Some already have one of our languages as their first (or second) language, and they find our ways familiar because in their countries of birth, similar government institutions developed from the same colonial roots.

This guide is prepared for family historians working in Canada, whose ancestors originated somewhere else. A few may have walked here over a land bridge a very long time ago, others may have flown into one of our major airports quite recently. We have many, varied pasts, but I hope some of these hints for time travellers will make your voyage more meaningful.

Chapter 1

A Time Traveller's Frame of Reference

Family historians are essentially time travellers. Your search quickly leads to the years before you were born; you explore your parents', your grandparents', and, with a little luck, their parents' and grandparents' worlds. Somewhere along the way you will discover that, "The past is a foreign country, they do things differently there." This telling statement opens the British novelist L.P. Hartley's *The Go-Between*, published in 1953.

1953 is not so long ago. In 1953 I was in my twenties and, as Maurice Chevalier sings in *Gigi*, "Ah yes, I remember it well" (at least I think I do). I can remember when the mailman came twice a day, when the postage on letters was 2¢ and postcards 1¢ — or have I been sorting through too many old family letters?

Of course, many readers were not yet born in 1953, and for you it is not part of your life, merely a recently past time you have been told about, but never experienced. I venture to suggest that this recent but unlived past is particularly dangerous for researchers, because it seems familiar in so many ways; we have been told about it by parents and grandparents, we have even seen it on TV, sometimes factually presented, but more often fictionalized. We think we recognize it, even though we never lived there ourselves.

Things change and people change with them. It's easy to make very wrong assumptions, even about life in the 1950s and '60s, because today's standards of what is politically correct and socially acceptable have changed. So has the technology we take for granted.

As you travel back in time, particularly through the early twentieth and late nineteenth centuries, you can quite suddenly find yourself in a world where some familiar convenience that you have taken for granted all your life does not exist. You have encountered my "first law of technology."

The First Law of Technology

There are dates *before which* certain things cannot exist because the technology was not known.

- There is usually a nebulous decade or two when any particular process is being developed and experimented with; let's call it the patent-pending period. However, unless your ancestors were inventors, scientists, or engineers they probably won't have been aware of the new toy.

- Towards the end of the patent-pending period, when the final form or forms of the technology are falling into place, enthusiastic amateurs discover it and start to play with it. That might be your uncle, who bought a kit and assembled an Altair 8800 hobby computer in 1975, or a great-grandfather who started taking photographs using wet-plate negatives in 1852.

- A period of popularization will follow, in which the new technology catches on and everyone wants one, be it an iPod, shares in the new railway, or a Daguerreotype of one's true love. In this interval, watch out for booms, bubbles, then crashes when the fad ends or the bubble bursts.

There is no such thing as an expiration date. A technology does not drop out of use and vanish simply because it is no longer "state of the art." Photography did not eliminate painting and drawing. Sewing by hand did not end when the sewing machine was invented. The older ways of doing things become romantic (like candles), artistic, and expensive handicrafts, or costly hobbies: what is written on a floppy disc or recorded on an Edison cylinder can be very difficult to access, unless you collect the now antique hardware and, for computers, the software to run it.

Five Revolutions in Technology

The past two centuries have seen new technologies change the way we live with ever increasing speed. They also changed the way we earn our wages, as well as what we spend them on.

As you go back in time to the Industrial Revolution in the last third of the eighteenth century, it may prove helpful to have a general framework for understanding the new and important technologies that earlier generations had to manage without.

In 2009, I came across such a framework presented in Carlota Perez's *Technological Revolutions and Financial Capital*, published in 2002.[1] Perez lists five technological revolutions:

1. **1771 — The Industrial Revolution** started in Britain when Richard Arkwright built the first successful water-powered cotton-spinning mill. Some might dispute this date, preferring 1769 when James Watt (1736–1819) patented his steam engine, an improved variant on Newcomen's steam-powered pumps (1712) used to remove water from coal mines.

2. **1829 — The Age of Steam and Railways** started in Britain, spreading to Europe and the U.S., was launched by the test of the "Rocket" steam engine for the Liverpool-Manchester railway at Rainhill in October 1829.

3. **1875 — The Age of Steel, Electricity, and Heavy Engineering** started when the Carnegie Bessemer process steel plant opened in Pittsburg in 1875, and the U.S. and Germany begin to overtake Britain, though Sir Henry Bessemer (1813–98) was British.

4. **1908 — The Age of Oil, the Automobile, and Mass Production** started in the U.S. (with Germany vying for world leadership) when the first Model T came out of the Ford plant in Detroit in 1908.

5. **1971 — The Age of Information and Telecommunication** started in the U.S., and spread to Europe and Asia. It was initiated in 1971 when the Intel microprocessor was introduced in Santa Clara, California.

About the time this outline was published, the iPod and smart phone appeared on the scene. Dare I suggest another revolution is on its way? **The Age of Mobile Internet Communication and Cloud Computing.**

2002–1971

If you are reading this book on paper, you have already moved back in time, prior to Perez's fifth age. This stage began in 1971 when computer technologies started to produce desktop, personal-use machines.

- Computers evolved during the Second World War, when they were used for code breaking. These room-sized mainframe computers were also top secret.

- Once the war ended, the technology was released for commercial use, but it was expensive and complex; few people understood it.

- Over the next two decades the read/write disk drive, the video display terminal (VDT), the mouse, and various proprietary programming software were developed and came together with the Intel microprocessor in 1971. Personal computers began to appear on desks.

- By the early 1980s, the Internet was taking form as a fast and convenient way for scientists and academics to communicate. The end of that decade brought the World Wide Web, and the 1990s saw computer users around the world going online.

If you are younger than 40 years of age, you are going to have to exercise your historical imagination when you travel back before 1970. In that world there were no easy-to-use personal computers, no public Internet — no Google.

1970–1908

Since we live in an era of mass production, oil, and automobiles, these related technologies are familiar, and will be a comfortable framework as you travel back in time to the years before the First World War. However, I am going to divide Perez's fourth revolution into two parts: after the Second World War (1936–1945) and before.

After the war: 1970–1945

Family historians who travel back in time will find that the end of the war in 1945 brought new modes of transportation, such as flying, and new technologies, like television.

- Post-war transportation changed radically, and as the 1950s moved into the 1960s, improved highways, throughways, interchanges, and expressways made the automobile the easy way to travel shorter distances.

- When the war ended, the Air Force veterans ("fly boys") came home and took over. Trains and ships still ran, but by the early 1950s, flying was how many people crossed the Atlantic or got from Montreal to Vancouver.

- Cable and telegraph gave way to radio, then telephone links to distant points. The first trans-Atlantic telephone cable was laid in 1956, and on 26 September that year, the *New York Times* reported the "First Call Made by Phone to Europe" and "Line's Capacity is 3 Times as Great as Radiophone's."[2] On the same day, similar stories appeared in newspapers throughout Canada.

- The BBC was broadcasting television in 1936, and in the U.S., RCA was experimenting, but all this was halted by the war. However, in 1949, television became widely available. In fact, by 1950, I was operating a television camera in a closed-circuit demonstration at the Canadian National Exhibition in Toronto.

- Later that year, Marconi TV cameras (run by Canadians) were broadcasting from the United Nations General Assembly on Long

Island. Finally in August 1952, the CBC, which held a monopoly, offered Canadians television from stations in Montreal and Toronto.

- Tape recording and magnetic recording tape were developed in Germany, captured in 1945 and brought to America as the profits of war. By 1948 they were being made commercially in the USA. In Canada in 1948, Utah Electronics started producing "portable" tape recorders; they were the size of a large carry-on suitcase.

- The war changed women's positions in universities, as many male professors left and were replaced, reluctantly, by highly qualified women. Some remained as full professors after the men returned. Throughout the war, girls with decent marks were encouraged to enter science, though engineering and architecture remained largely male-dominated professions.

- In 1960, oral contraceptives were first marketed. The pill gave women certain and convenient control over their bodies and greater sexual freedom.

- Air freight and faster highway transportation changed how fish, meat, fruit, and vegetables were distributed and what was freshly available in the new supermarkets. Quick, convenient frozen food had also arrived by 1948.

- Credit cards began to be accepted by many merchants, which changed shopping habits. The big department stores lost their dominant position.

Before the War: 1936–1908

These years saw the First World War, the Great Depression, and in between, the Jazz Age. By 1930, T. H. Raddall (1903–94) had written of "things and people and a way of life that were passing rapidly, for the 1914–18 war and its tremendous effects were changing everything."[3] Raddall operated a wireless telegraph (radio) at sea during the war, which had become mandatory on all ships. Marconi's invention is only one of then-new technologies still with us.

By 1908, we not only had the Model T, but flying had become possible on both sides of the Atlantic. Moving pictures brought *Pathé News of the Week* to a paying audience. Escalators were installed in department stores and the London underground.

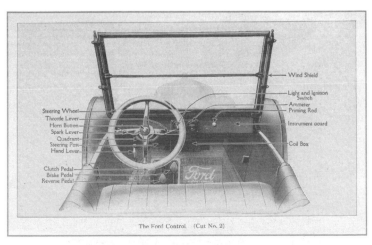

Driving a Model T was very different from "Dobbin" and the buggy. This 1921 Canadian edition of the Ford Manual *tried to explain everything*

A fascinating window on this rapidly changing world is offered by Juliet Nicolson's *The Perfect Summer*, a study of England in the summer of 1911, when King George V was crowned.[4] As his reign continued, more and more families across Europe and North America came to own an automobile, a machine that played recorded sound, a hand-held camera to take snapshots, and, after 1920, a radio. Broadcasting as we know it developed gradually.

- Reginald Fessenden made the first radio broadcast of voice and music on Christmas Eve 1906, startling the Marconi Company's operators who had only heard Morse code on their wireless receivers at shore stations and on ships at sea. Telegrapher's Morse Code was finally discontinued in the late 1990s.

- The Marconi Wireless Company opened the first public broadcasting stations in Britain in February 1920, followed by XWA (the Canadian Branch of Marconi Wireless) in Montreal on 20 May 1920 (that November, it became CFCF). The first American station, KDKA in Pittsburg, did not sign on until November 1920.

- The Canadian Radio Broadcasting Commission, which later became the CBC, was an outgrowth of the Canadian National Railway's early experiments with radio entertainment for train passengers. The CRBC began broadcasting in both French and English from Montreal in May 1933.

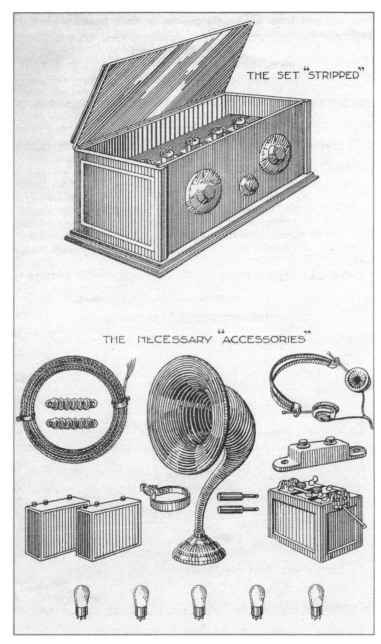

THE SET "STRIPPED"

THE NECESSARY "ACCESSORIES"

By 1926 "broadcast receivers" were being used by thousands of people, and women were "becoming ardent radio users." From MacLean's Radio Manual, which offered information for "people who are more interested in results than in scientific theory."

At first, electricity was an urban service. Where it was available, households began to use a variety of small and inexpensive appliances: irons, toasters, single or double hot plates, and fans all became electric. More costly but equally desirable new electric appliances were vacuum cleaners, washing machines, and electric refrigerators to replace the old ice-boxes. The ice-man and ice-making companies gradually went the way of the buggy whip.

As new technologies are accepted and drive out older services and products, you may find that your ancestors also got caught up in the enthusiastic adoption of a new innovation boom, or that their existing technologies were being replaced. Here are two examples. My uncle Lonzo McCoy got into the postcard business both as a printer and owner of several Postcard Shops just as the fad started in 1900. However, booms are followed by busts, and by 1910 he had closed his printing business due to lagging postcard sales.[5] Then there's the story of my husband's great-uncle Ed. He once had a very profitable ice business in New York City, but by the mid-1930s his ice-making business floundered with the popularity of refrigerators, and he came home to the Eastern Townships in Quebec to live with his nieces.

1908–1875

The generation that grew up between 1875 and 1908 saw incredible changes in the way we live. Bessemer's steel processes revolutionized the industry, and electric light illuminated the urban world. Automobiles became available, but only as toys for the rich. This was a world where most transportation was by horse power, steam railways, steamships, or steam-driven barges on rivers and canals.

- There are still horses around, but they are no longer the primary form of transportation or power they were before 1908.

- Electric lights, as we know them, did not exist until Thomas Edison patented the carbon filament bulb in 1879. Joseph Swan had been working on the filament problem since 1860 in England; he solved it at about the same time as Edison, and in the process, invented an artificial silk. Neither inventor's "glow lamps" ended the use of candles, though, which were invented by the Phoenicians.[6]

- These were also the years when thousands of people poured into North America from all parts of Europe. Most arrived by steamship, and the new railways carried them west across the new Dominion of Canada.

- Long distance communication was done by post, telegraph, or cable. Samuel Morse demonstrated a workable telegraph system in 1837. After an attempt in 1857, which was only operational for two months, the first trans-Atlantic cable was successfully laid by the *Great Eastern* in 1866. Limited telephone systems existed, as well, and Alexander Graham Bell patented the technology in 1876.

These are also years where we begin to find photographs, which can help us visualize our ancestors and how they

lived. Photography began around 1840, developed further during the 1850s (the tintype was patented in 1856),
and became simpler and easier for amateurs by 1880 with
Eastman's dry-plate negatives.

*Portion of a letter sent from Scotland in 1857 to James Douglas in West
Farnham, Canada East, noting that "Cable is now through to America and the
Queen has more than once sent a message through & got an answer back. So you
can send a telligraph message now it will save writing...."*

1875–1829

Move back in time before the 1870s, and about the only
familiar technologies are steam-powered: the railways are
primitive, the steamboats picturesque. The world is lit by
oil lamps or gas, there is some early photography, and you
can listen to "recorded" music played on wind-up music
boxes or player pianos.

> • When you try to imagine how most people
> lived in the mid-nineteenth century, try to
> remember any weekends you might have
> spent at some log cabin in the woods, where

there was no electricity, where running water came through a pipe from an uphill spring, and a wood-burning stove provided heat, hot water, and any meals you were able to cook on it.

- In cities, most homes did not have running water. They depended on a common tap or pump. Running water is required to make indoor plumbing possible. Joseph Bramah's valve closet, a toilet bowl that maintained a water seal to prevent cesspool smells from entering the room, was patented in 1778, but it wasn't until mid-Victorian times that most households had such "newfangled" conveniences.

- Oil-burning lamps and candles lit homes, and were far more efficient than those the Romans used. Gas, distilled from coal, was used for lighting public streets in London as early as 1807; by 1819 gas street lighting was common in several cities, and was also used in shops and public buildings. However, because of the heat and smell, gas did not become widely used in private homes until the latter half of the century, and, in 1879, Edison's carbon-filament light bulb made safer electric light possible.

- Labour-saving machines, many hand- or foot-powered, became available to help with domestic and agricultural tasks. The sewing machine is a typical example of one such machine. Many sewing machines were patented beginning in the late eighteenth century, the most workable of which were chain-stitch types, meant for use on leather. The first lock-stitch machine was patented in the United States in 1846. In 1857, the first commercially successful sewing machine was designed and built by Isaac Merrit Singer (1811–1875), after which machine sewing, as opposed to hand sewing, came into common use. Making the clothes for a large family became a lot easier.

1829–1771

The Industrial Revolution began in Britain where, by the eighteenth century, labour costs were high but energy, from both water-power and cheap coal, was readily available. The great inventions of that century — the steam engine, mechanical spinning, smelting iron with coke — all served to save money on wages, the most costly factor of production, by using energy produced by something other than human or animal muscle power.[7]

- The eighteenth century saw major changes in agricultural methods. This freed workers to go work in factories, and, in Britain, the bulk of the working population moved from agriculture to industry. The textile industry is an early example of industrialization, creating a demand for machines and tools to make these machines, leading to further mechanization.

- For centuries, water had been driving grain-grinding mills. These mills had to be located where there was high-pressure water flow but locating factories beside waterfalls is not always convenient.

- In 1769, James Watt (1736–1819) patented his steam-engine, a much improved variant of Newcomen's steam-powered pumps (1712), which had been developed to remove water from coal mines.

- Sir Richard Arkwright (1732–92) was a pioneer of cotton spinning. His first small mill (1767) in Nottingham used horse power. The second, in Cromford, Derbyshire (1771), used water power to run what became known as "water frames." A mill he built in Manchester in 1781–82 attempted using the Newcomen steam engine to run the machinery, and when this didn't work he used the engine to pump water from a lower pond to one at a higher level from which it could flow onto a water wheel that ran the factory. Steam power brought the waterfall to the factory.[8]

- As a result, factories could now be located in urban areas where more workers lived.

That first Industrial Revolution required improved transportation, provided by canals, roads, railways, and steamships. As machinery was developed to facilitate this work, engineers and workers became more technically skilled. These skills were exported to other countries and throughout the Empire, making Britain the most powerful industrial country in the world for some decades. It also radically changed the face of British society, as large cities were quickly built (particularly in the Midlands) as people left the countryside.

Life Before These Revolutions

And so we have moved back in time through pre-Confederation Canada, through Jane Austen's England, to Loyalist British North America. There are fewer and fewer familiar technologies in this increasingly foreign country, but we can get some idea of what life was like in the eighteenth and nineteenth centuries, more readily perhaps than life in 1911 or 1940.

- Almost anywhere you wander there are "historic" houses, or even complete villages where the past is preserved for our amusement or education. Sometimes there are also reenactments mirroring local historical events.

- It's easy to find reality shows (mostly from the BBC) in which modern people, often historians and archaeologists, try to live like families did in some other era. Among the latest are the BBC's *Tales from the Green Valley*, which shows us how people lived and farmed in 1620, with a second program covering a year on a Victorian farm, with machinery (steam, hand, or horse-driven) and more modern conveniences.

- One intriguing element in both the historic villages and the television series are the number of experts they have found who know how to use old tools and machinery, specialize in old building techniques, or can play the music and dance the dances our ancestors did.

Shortcuts

As you track your families back through history, some people or certain events will almost certainly intrigue you and you will want to know more about the world they lived in. You can search for information on the Internet, read books, both fiction and non-fiction, or watch television or movies. What each tells you may or may not be accurate. Each have certain caveats as to facts and exactness.

- If you can find a novel set in the time and place you are interested in, by an author of the same time and place, writing for readers of their period (Charles Dickens or Jane Austen, for example) you should be able to learn a lot from casual references to what characters were using, doing, and buying. These kinds of details will be accurate, based as they are on common knowledge of the time.
- Published diaries or collected letters — and there are a lot these days — provide a detailed glimpse of a specific historical time

and place. You will find references to some in the following chapters.

• Scholarly biographies are not always the dull reading one might fear, and a good biographer usually introduces the reader to the world of their subject in the first chapter or two. They are well worth dipping into for a view of a specific past.

• If such biographies or novels have been made into a movie or TV series, remember that the facts of the period have been passed through a modern filter as the story has been condensed.

> **Warning**: Historical accuracy in period costumes and settings only became important after the Second World War, starting in Britain in the 1950s with stage productions of classics. By then researchers and historians were publishing detailed historical information, along with better and more accurate illustrations. More directors, designers, and technicians had academic training, and so demanded historically accurate costumes and sets. Just compare the costumes worn by the women in the 1940 film of *Pride and Prejudice* with those worn in the 1995 BBC series.

- Although recent BBC series based on novels and biographies tend to be quite accurate, anachronisms do slip in. Movies are considerably more suspect: cinematographers get the artistic bit between their teeth and characters do things they never would have done. War films made during the Second World War are probably visually correct, but watch out for propaganda of the more optimistic sort.

- If your time travel takes you back to England in the late-eighteenth to late-nineteenth centuries, an all-encompassing guide book is Daniel Pool's *What Jane Austen Ate and Charles Dickens Knew: From Fox Hunting to Whist — The Facts of Daily Life in 19th-century England*. The 135-page glossary is your Berlitz vocabulary, the 255-page first part will instruct you on all the social niceties and advise you on what to avoid.[9]

The following chapters cannot begin to cover all the unfamiliar ways of life you will encounter as you move into the past, but they may remind you of some of the things we are forgetting, like the guinea and the farthing, the peck and the perch, and some lesser known details of our heritage. You will find information on older technologies like the horse and carriage, and a lot of dates and events that could have motivated your ancestors to change where they lived or find a new way to earn their living. *Bon voyage!*

Chapter 2

Dealing with Documents

Eighteenth and Nineteenth Century Documents

Most Respected Reader,

I humbly beseech you not to be annoyed or offended by the formal, not to say obsequious language that was the standard polite form for petitions, legal documents, and even some private letters up until the twentieth century. That is how it was done.

In the past, as in the future,
Please be assured, Honoured Sir or Madame,
I remain Your Most Humble
and obd^{t} Servt.
The Author

Deference to Power

Most of what we know about our past is based on information in letters and documents that have survived from earlier times. We may laugh when we read something like the letter on the previous page today, but not too long ago it was the standard form and perfectly appropriate. It should remind you that there has always been a pyramid of power.[1]

Always consider the hierarchy. Even today people write differently to their superiors, their equals, or those they supervise. Three letters from the same official could tell quite different stories depending on the rank of the recipient.

What Survives Where?

The first challenge is to find those letters. Historical records, even vital statistics, are neither created nor kept for the benefit of genealogists or family historians.

- Most official records have been created and kept because they involve the ownership of property, or the receipt or payment of money.

- In the past the best records were maintained by large, hierarchical institutions such as government departments, established churches, and commercial enterprises that could afford to compile the data they needed, then store it for a century or two. Only recently has the computer changed that. Now we must hope that archives and libraries maintain both the hardware and software necessary for viewing texts and pictures that might have only been produced a decade or two earlier.

- Records are created, copied, and kept, at different administrative levels in any institution, for example:

  ○ archdiocese, diocese, or parish

  ○ head office, factory, branch plant, or sales agent

  ○ federal, provincial, county, township, or municipal governments

  ○ Some may be international, because colonial officials sent copies back to "head office" in the mother country.

  A Word of Warning: Many official records were indexed as they were made, if only as a matter of self-preservation, by some lowly clerk. However, more than one index may exist, and they may not agree.[2] When you find a list or index of names, be suspicious. Ask who was indexing what, when, and for what purpose.

- There might be copies that were made at the time, or a later date.
- Each signatory of a treaty or contract usually gets a copy.

  ○ Letters, petitions, and lists might be sent to several people.

- Some churches that kept civil records had to send a copy to a higher authority, for example bishops' transcripts.

- Did some earlier scholar see the gravestones or documents before they were lost, and make copies or notes as to the contents? Ask at the local library.

Finding records is only the first challenge. You then have to look at them, read them, and interpret them. A thorough discussion of this is a book in itself, and some very useful advice can be found in Brenda Merriman's *Genealogy in Ontario*.[3]

Writing

Ink and paper may be becoming an obsolete form of conveying knowledge, but if books, letters and records escape fire, flood, mice, mould, and destructive people, they tend to survive and remain readable. Michael E. Fitton's recent article "It Is Written"[4] surveys the physical elements of documents, and touches briefly on handwriting. However language changes, customs change, and it is easy to misinterpret what our ancestors wrote down.

The First Rule of Research: Never trust a transcript made by someone else. Wherever you can, check the original document.

Medieval and Elizabethan writing is difficult for the average person to read, unless you've taken a course in palaeography. On the other hand, when researchers encounter documents from the eighteenth and early nineteenth century, the writing looks so much like our own that the tendency is to plunge in — right into an orthographic trap. Here are a few traps you should watch out for:

- Old fashioned writing habits persisted in North America long after they disappeared in Britain and France, perhaps because there were fewer teachers, and those that there were often stuck to the old ways and could influence a second and even third generation.

- Many of us recognize the long *s* that looks like an *f* when it appears in print (ſ). However, when it turns up in handwritten text, it is easily misread as a *p* or *l,* since it persisted when writing a double *s,* long after it was dropped from most type fonts.

  An Example: *Cafs, Cap, Cals* or *Cass?* Looking for a family named Cass in published indexes of parish registers of eastern Ontario and western Quebec, I found that Cass had not only been read and indexed as Carr, but since several priests had used the old-fashioned long-short double ss, Ca*f*s also turned up as Cap and once as Cals.

West Farnham
March 11th 1861

My dear Mr Douglafs

I should have been out to see you, but I have been told that the roads are very bad, and being obliged to walk I have unwillingly failed to visit you. I hope you are now quite recovered from your late sicknefs, and that you are not unthankful to Almighty God for your restoration to health. I inclose twenty-six shillings and nine pence, being the balance of what I owe you for the butter. There were in all 51 lbs at eleven pence, and the price was there

This letter, written 11 March 1861 in West Farnham, Canada East, shows the older long f s at the end of Douglaf s and again in sicknef s. Note that in 1861 the money in use was still pounds, shillings, and pence, not dollars and cents.

- When a letter or two are written as super-script at the end of a word, it usually signified a contraction or abbreviation. *Y*, the old form of "the," was going out of fashion by the middle of the eighteenth century but wth and wch are quite common. "John" may appear as *J*^{n} or *J*^{no}, but be careful not to confuse these with *Jo*^{n} or *Jo*^{na} for "Jonathan." Remember *X* means "Christ" as "Xian" or "Xopher" (Christopher) or "Xmas." It is also the Roman numeral for 10 (see chapter 4).

- Beware of the lazy parish clerk who uses "ditto" abbreviated to *D*^{o}. It was once read as December when it actually referred back to June a few lines above. As well, be suspicious of ditto marks used by census takers, particularly regarding origin or birthplace.

Spelling

Spelling in the eighteenth and nineteenth centuries was, for the most part, phonetic and highly variable. You can presume relatively literate usage in official government documents and reports, but the spelling of names is always variable — especially in Canada because of the mingling of French- and English-speaking language groups, plus local pockets of Gaelic, and various European and Asian languages. Since spelling was phonetic, you may even hear the echo of an ancestor's accent in the writing.

The Second Rule of Research: Always remember that clerks and clergymen, census takers and directory compilers, wrote down what they heard — what people said to them.

• Not all English speaking people use the Queen's English. We find variously accented English spoken in North America and across much of Asia, as well as in Australia and New Zealand. In earlier centuries, settlers from the British Isles brought a variety of broad local dialects across the Atlantic.

> **An Example**: Imagine the potential in 1776 for misunderstanding, and misspellings, when an upper-class British officer who wanted repairs made at Fort Cumberland in Nova Scotia engaged a newly arrived stonemason speaking broadest Yorkshire, a carpenter born and raised in Connecticut, and perhaps a couple of Acadian labourers whose first language was French!

• In rural French Canada, until almost the end of the nineteenth century, the priest, seigneur, and notary were usually the only ones who could write. The original Loyalists and emigrants from England or Scotland could usually sign their name with a flourish, but their children, growing up in settlements without schoolmasters might well sign with "His *X* Mark" or "Her *X* Mark."

- A century ago, even if someone could sign his or her name, he or she may not have been capable of reading and checking everything that was written down. Even today it is optimistic to assume everyone is fully literate.

Lost in Translation

In the past, when people left their country of birth for a place where a different language was spoken, their name would often change as well. Sometimes, spelling is changed to ensure a name is pronounced the same as it always was.

- In a French-speaking area, for example, spelling Douglas with a double *s*, i.e. "Douglass," allows Francophones to pronounce the name properly, instead of asking for "Madame Dooglah."

- In English-speaking areas, on the other hand, French names are often anglicized. If you do not know how Benoit is supposed to be pronounced, you may not recognize "Benwa" as a variant spelling. Hénault can become "Eno," Sauvé becomes "Sophy." They ensure much the same pronunciation, but English phonetic spelling.

- Immigrants from eastern Europe or the Orient presented a particular problem, since English- or French-speaking clerks might not have any idea of how a name should be spelled, particularly if the immigrant's documents were in the Greek or Cyrillic alphabets, Arabic, or an Oriental script.

• If the original name is long, consider how it might be shortened. I once found a sequence of directory entries where a family from central Europe first appeared as "Tatarachuk," then "Tarchuk," and finally as "Tarc." Clearly, the family dropped syllables to make it easier to say and spell.

• If you do not speak your family's native language, and are not sure how the original family name was pronounced, find someone who does and ask for help. Look first for phonetic variants, but also consider what the name means. Translation was often the answer to names others could neither spell nor pronounce.

> **Examples**: Joseph Leblanc, when he moved to the Boston States may have become Joe White. A long search in England for a Madame Dubois ended when we found out that she was known there as Mrs. Wood. A friend once told me his family translated their Italian name, Campobello, to Beauchamp when they came to Quebec. Move Beauchamp to England and it becomes the familiar Beecham, of pill and conductor fame.

- Names tend to indicate nationality; at one time this could influence one's position in society. During the First World War, when Germany was "The Enemy," some families chose to make their name less German, translating Battenberg to Mountbatten, for example.

The Latin You Forgot

A century ago, when a proper education was based around Latin, school children were far more familiar with both Roman numerals (see chapter 4) and Latin words than adults are today. Expect to encounter Latin terms and abbreviations in historical documents.

- Newspapers and business documents often abbreviate dates:

"on the 15th ult."	(*ultimo*)	a date in the preceding month,
"on the 20th inst."	(instant)	[not Latin] the current month,
"on the 10th prox."	(*proximo*)	a date in the month to come.

- Abbreviations for the last four months of the year are based on the Latin names for the seventh to tenth months. They are more common in French texts ([bre]) than in English records ([ber]), but in either language, clerks or priests may use either Arabic or Roman numerals.

September (7bre, VIIber)	October (8ber, VIIIber),
November (9ber, IXbre),	December (10bre, Xber)

- Some abbreviations based on Latin are still used now and again.

  An Example: *c.* or *ca.* (*circa*), or *abt.* (about) are the standard abbreviations used for signalling a birth, marriage, or death date (e.g. "b. ca.1792"). These are used to show this date has been calculated from other evidence (e.g. age given in a census or obituary, which are always suspect).

  An Example: *eg.*, or *e.g.*, or *ex.gr.*, all are abbreviations for "for example," which comes from the Latin *exempli gratia*.

  An Example: *fl. ca.* 1735 means that someone *floruit circa* or flourished about 1735. This tells us an individual named in the particular record was clearly alive about that date (or dates), but neither birth nor death dates are known.

- When dealing with older indexes and catalogues, researchers often encounter other terms or abbreviations based on Latin.

An Example: *Liber*, or *Lib.*, meaning a bound volume, is used to indicate specific register volumes, usually with an identifying letter or number.

An Example: *Recto* (right side of a leaf) and *verso* (reverse side of a leaf) appear when registers are foliated, i.e. each leaf is numbered instead of each page. In the index, the two sides of a leaf will appear as 23r, 23v.

Postage before 1840

In Britain, the Royal Mail was established in 1512 and issued the world's first postage stamps in May 1840. Before that date the British postal service was surprisingly good, but the recipient paid the postage. The General Post Office (GPO — it became the Post Office Corporation in 1969) handled national and international mail and charged by the sheet, in addition to the distance carried.

- The size of the sheet of paper did not matter, the number of sheets did, so instead of envelopes, most letters were written on a single, large, folded sheet of paper, which was folded again and sealed, leaving a blank space on the back page for the address and postmarks.

- Postage was very expensive, except for the friends and relations of Members of Parliament and the House of Lords. They could "frank" letters, which were then delivered free of charge.

- In large cities like London, the two-penny post was organized and operated separately from the GPO. With two deliveries a day it was possible to send a note and receive a reply on the same day.

- Different postmarks were used for morning and afternoon delivery, and the various postmarks stamped on a letter that crossed an ocean show the route it took. Postmarks are a study in themselves.

Cross-writing

To cram as much news as possible on the single sheet, some nineteenth century letters were cross-written. There was skill to this, and it is often much easier to read than you might think at first glance. Relax, let your eyes follow the lines, and your brain will separate out the text.

Two Useful Conventions

There are two conventions accepted by scholars for transcribing handwritten manuscripts:

- Put pointed brackets < > around ambiguous or difficult to read words.

- Use square brackets [ ] to indicate the enclosed comments are your own, and not in the text being copied.

An Example: She told me her name was Al<ltaya>. [known to be: Althea]

Use these when making notes, you will bless yourself two years later.

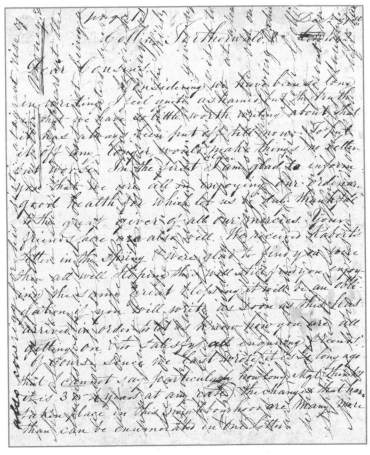

Legible cross-writing was a skill that saved paper and postage.

A Final Word of Warning

Wherever possible, check the original source. You could do that up to about 1980, then came Bill Gates, Steve Jobs, and the Internet. I wrote my thesis without a computer. It was literally cut and paste, type and retype, giving thanks for corrasable bond paper. Snowpak was invented in 1951, but forbidden on a thesis to be preserved in the library. Now all that is obsolete, but a hundred years from now you will still be able to read that typed thesis if it survives as ink on paper. The digital software I am using to write this book is already obsolete, and you cannot read these words I am typing unless I print them out or transfer them to different software.

* * *

Useful Published Sources

Elizabeth Briggs, *Handbook for Reading & Interpreting Old Documents; With examples from The Hudson's Bay Company Archives* (Winnipeg: Manitoba Genealogical Society, 1992) is particularly useful if you are working with numerical accounts. It also has a brief guide to unfamiliar terms and conventions from the past.

Chapter 3

Dealing with Family Tradition

U.E. or D.A.R.?

My roots are all in the Maritimes, and they are entangled with many families' traditions. When we moved to Toronto in 1981, I decided that I should apply to become a United Empire Loyalist; surely one or two of those late-comers had married into my family tree. They had, but as my research revealed, there were problems. A long-held family tradition of "Loyalist descent" is not acceptable genealogical proof of such descent.

- Marriage records in many parts of what became New Brunswick are thin on the ground. I had the petition of a soldier, who settled on the Mirimichi, proving he was a Loyalist — but his marriage was unrecorded.

- Westmorland County had better records. One of the Chapmans from Yorkshire married a Margaret Weldon "and her ancestors on the maternal side — the Killams — were United Empire Loyalists."[1] That quote is from a Chapman entry in *A Cyclopedia of Canadian Biography.* In the same volume was an entry for an Amasa Emerson Killam, also claiming the Killams were Loyalists.

- These entries, all of course backed by "family tradition," showed a Loyalist claim made by two branches of the family, one of them repeating it in the *Biographical Review: this volume contains biographical sketches of leading citizens of the province of New Brunswick,*[2] with impressive details, though no proof.

- Alas, these claims were not true. Research showed Amasa Killam was a Planter, a pre-Revolutionary settler from the New England colonies who supported the Eddy Rebellion and was paid by the state of Massachusetts. It seems I might qualify as a Daughter of the American Revolution.

I have gone on at length about the Killams in part to show you how family traditions can become "mythinformation," distorting actual historical facts, particularly where politics were involved. Both the Killams and the Chapmans were in politics, and for a nineteenth century politician in New Brunswick, Loyalist roots were politically very correct.

Must It Be True?

Surely entries in the family Bible must be true? Don't be too sure. First, check the date of publication compared to the dates of the first entries. If the Bible was published some years *after* the dates of the first entries they may have been copied (or miscopied) into the new Bible from some other source.

- Be suspicious if several entries over many years are all in the same ink. The handwriting may be the same, but different inks indicate different times of writing, and so are probably contemporary with the event recorded.

     An Example: There is a Bible in my family, published some years after the dates of the first entries, that records one date that does not agree with the parish register. Counting the months between the marriage and the first birth often explains the difference.

- "But Grandmother told me." — Family lore, when handed down over several generations, is subject to human error from poor memories. Nevertheless, most tales contain a grain of truth. Family myths frequently substitute a better-known name or event for one with a similar sound, spelling, or location.

> **An Example:** My mother used to tell me the Chapmans, who arrived in Nova Scotia in 1774, came from Haddon Hall. Looking into family history, I learned that Haddon Hall was an ancient and famous castle in Derbyshire. The Chapmans lived at Hawnby Hall (the New Hall), a modest grey stone Georgian house on the outskirts of Hawnby, a small village in the North Riding of Yorkshire. The names of both Halls begin with "H."

Living Where?

The past holds a number of toponymic traps, the most common being several places with the same name. When your grandmother said "Saint John" did she mean Saint John, New Brunswick; St. John's, Newfoundland; or St. Johns (now Saint-Jean-sur-Richelieu), Quebec? They can sound very similar when your grandmother was reminiscing. St. John could even be the township in the Cochrane District of Ontario, or — it could refer to the river.

- Think of the importance of rivers to early settlers. When your grandmother said "Ottawa" or "Saint John," did her family actually live "along" or "up" or "beside" the river of that name? Such meaningful words can drop out of memory over a century and leave you with a puzzling reference to Richelieu, Rideau, or Rhine. Remember, as well, that more than one river has given its name to a whole area, in Canada most commonly where lumbering was the primary industry.

• Cities tend to swallow their suburbs. Great-aunt Mary, talking to family members from Toronto or Edmonton, may say she was born, or lived in Montreal, when actually the family lived in Verdun or Pointe-Claire or even across the river in Longueuil.

• A relative born in the suburbs of Montreal, or London, Moscow, Rome, Berlin, Beijing, or Budapest, explaining to someone who has never been there how a suburb relates to the better-known city may have difficulties. It is so much easier to name the large, well-known place. Knowing the family's church or mosque or synagogue could be the clue to discovering where they actually lived, and where to look for census and other records.

• In some cities various areas have unofficial names that the locals use. Someone from the island of Montreal may live on the Lakeshore or the West Island, in Toronto, Cabbagetown and Yorkville have become chic addresses, New York has Harlem and shares Soho with London. If the nickname has a slightly derogatory connotation, look for downtown areas where immigrants first settled (e.g. Cabbagetown). Lakeshore, The Beaches, English Bay, or Britannia Bay may formerly have been waterside cottage colonies close to the city, once inexpensive housing, but now anything but.

Religion and Language *Prove* Nothing

No matter what your great-grandmother adamantly denied, or insisted was true, be suspicious and check the other side of the religious and language divides wherever and whatever they may be: Roman Catholic and Protestant, French and English, Aboriginal and European.

- Until well into the twentieth century, churches were the social centres in communities. These were the places where different groups of migrants met and got to know each other even though they spoke different languages. Until very recently in any culture with Two Solitudes, more often than not these are based on religion, not on language. A "mixed marriage" usually meant a Catholic to a Protestant, but in some communities it could be a Baptist to an Anglican.

- A Roman Catholic parish may include some, or even a majority, of Irish or Highland Scots immigrants. In the Ottawa Valley immigrants from Bavaria and Poland also went to the Catholic church, and married into the other language groups.

- Some Protestant congregations, despite being primarily English-speaking, included people with French-sounding names who came from the Channel Islands, or were Huguenot; or in Nova Scotia, French or German speaking "Foreign Protestants."

- For much of the nineteenth and twentieth centuries, any Aboriginal ancestor (almost always a woman) was something to be hidden and denied. Now of course, people are far less reticent to prove Aboriginal blood.

- Any Aboriginal blood I can claim has been well diluted over two centuries: a river pilot, John Touchie, who came to the Mirimichi around 1775 is believed to have had a wife who was Mi'kmaq. There is no proof, only circumstantial evidence; in a long-settled region like New Brunswick, everyone knew who everyone's grandparents were. Such facts of racial origin were known, but rarely mentioned.

- The census of 1851–52 in Quebec had a separate column for the enumerator to indicate if anyone was "Negro" or "Indian," but this was probably only filled in if someone looked non-white. However, there were children, both legitimate and illegitimate, of mixed race. The community knew, but it was not spoken of and rarely recorded.

Social Differences

Researchers must be alert to the importance of different social statuses, as well as ever-changing social customs. Family traditions often distort such matters, and there is usually an upwards shift. That is a hazard for the modern time traveller — particularly the younger and more egalitarian of you.

> **An Example**: At the turn of the twenty-first century, I can talk quite freely about my Mi'kmaq ancestry, about a great-great-grandfather who was a bigamist, a great-grandfather who went bankrupt, and a grandfather who was a boiler-maker. At the turn of the last century, the first three would have been shameful secrets, the working-class skilled tradesman quietly ignored.

Social class divisions change with place and time and in earlier eras were far more rigid than they are today. Regardless, social mobility did exist, and Britain was more accommodating than most of Europe. From Chaucer's day to the present, money, talent, charm, and a good etiquette book all helped.

- Etiquette books were not written for the people who knew how to behave in polite society, but for those who aspired to be accepted. In 1577 Hugh Rodes was advising:

  > Blow not your nose on the napkin
  > where you should wype your hande;
  > Fyll not thy mouth to full, leaste
  > thou perhaps of force must speake;

Dip not thy meate in the Saltseller,
but take it with thy knyfe.

- For the twentieth century, try to find an edition of Gertrude Pringle's *Etiquette in Canada: The Blue Book of Social Usage* (1932), or one of Emily Post's pronouncements on etiquette from the first decades of this century, perhaps in your grandmother's attic.

- I've recommended Daniel Pool's *What Jane Austen Ate and Charles Dickens Knew: From Fox Hunting to Whist — The Facts of Daily Life in Nineteenth-Century England* (1993) as an excellent all purpose guidebook on how society worked in the past. Most of it applies to nineteenth century Canada, too.

- "Courtesy books" are now treasured in rare book collections, and have been digitized and made available on the Internet. You may also find early books on household management, cookery, eighteenth century ideas for raising children, or the steps of the quadrille that began early nineteenth century balls.

- Modern books and articles also explain every aspect of life in the past: courtship, domestic service, medicine, travel, and trades of all sorts. There are many magazines dedicated to social history, which are particularly rich sources for family historians.

Chapter 4

What Every Schoolchild Used to Know

Researchers frequently encounter Roman numerals when trying to determine the publication dates of older books.

Numerals			
Arabic	Roman	Arabic	Roman
1	I	20	XX
2	II	21	XXI
3	III	25	XXV
4	IV	50	L
5	V	100	C
6	VI	300	CCC
7	VII	500	D
8	VIII	555	DLV
9	IX	700	DCC

10	X	900	CM or DCCCC
11	XI	1000	M
13	XIII	1492	MCDXCII
14	XIV	1769	MDCCLXIX
15	XV	1867	MDCCCLXVII
16	XVI	1999	MCMXCIX
19	XIX	2000	MM

Metrication

The metric system has not been with us all that long. It is a product of the French Revolution and the use of it was made compulsory in France in 1801. Canada tried to make it compulsory in the 1970s.

- Metrication was a slow and unpopular process, starting with weather reports switching over to Celsius from Fahrenheit.

- In 1977, the kilogram replaced the pound in the retail food industry. The process took over two years as all commercial scales were converted. Many customers refused to convert, and prices are still posted "per pound" as well as "per kilogram," perhaps because the price per kilo seems much higher than by the pound,

- Gasoline and oil sales changed from gallons to litres, and road signs and speed limits from miles to kilometres, over "a two-year period beginning January 1, 1979."[1] This was more readily accepted, probably

because the price per litre looked so much
lower and speeds appeared to be faster.

Before Metrication

After nearly two decades of using the metric system, we no
longer find equivalency tables for the old imperial system
correlating bushels and pecks, gallons and quarts, rods, furlongs, and fathoms, printed on the back of school exercise
books or in pocket diaries.

- **Before the French Revolution:** Until
  Napoleon spread the metric system across
  Europe, most countries had their own
  units of measurement. Some of those used
  in France and New France are listed below,
  but the distance a "mile" or "league" repre-
  sents depends on what country you are in.

  An Example: A map of Switzerland
  published by Robert Sayer in 1774
  has five scale bars showing leagues
  of Switzerland, common miles of
  Italy, common miles of Germany,
  common French leagues, and
  English statute miles.

- **Imperial Long Measure:** Any older English
  maps you consult will have scale given in
  imperial units, such as 1 inch to 1 mile, or 1
  inch to 4 miles, but you may also meet less
  familiar units, such as 1 inch to 40 chains,
  1 inch to 16 chains, or a scale bar showing

miles and furlongs. In case you are not sure about units of length and land measurement, the tables below give two versions of the standardized units of the eighteenth through the twentieth centuries:[2]

(From a school scribbler)	
12 lines	1 inch
4 inches	1 hand
12 inches	1 foot
3 feet	1 yard
6 feet	1 fathom
5½ yards	1 rod or pole
40 rods	1 furlong
8 furlongs	1 mile
3 miles	1 league
69½ miles	1 degree
1,760 yards	1 mile
5,280 feet	1 mile
6,075.81 feet	1 nautical mile *
Mariners' Measure	
1 fathom	6 feet
1 cable length	120 fathoms
*1 international nautical mile	6,076.11 feet

*The nautical mile is 1 minute of longitude measured along the equator, a distance about which a number of opinions are held. The British Admiralty measured mile is 6,080 feet (1.852 kilometres).[3]

Linear Measure and Metric Equivalents	
1 foot	12 inches = 304.8mm/30.48 cm
1 yard	3 feet = 0.9144 metres
1 rod/perch/pole	16.5 feet
1 rod/perch/pole	5.5 yards = 5.029 metres
1 furlong/*rood*	40 rods/(1/8 mile) = 201.16 metres
1 furlong/*rood*	660 feet/220 yards
1 statute mile	5,280 feet/1760 yards
1 statute mile	8 furlongs
3 land miles	1 league
Irish mile (obs.)	2,240 yards
Scots mile (obs.)	976 yards (approx.)

Surveying and Land Measure

Let's start with a few definitions of some commonly used terms.

- **chain**, n. ... (9) *Survey* **a**. a measuring instrument consisting of 100 wire rods or links, each 7.92 inches long (surveyor's or Gunter's chain), or one foot long (engineer's chain). **b**. the length of a surveyor's chain (66 feet) or engineer's chain (100 feet).

- **chain-man**, n. (pl.-men), a man who holds the chain in making surveying measurements.

- **rod** n. ... (4) a stick used to measure with. (5) a linear measure of 5½ yards or 16½ feet, a perch or pole. (6) a square perch or pole (30¼ square yards).[4]

Gunter's or surveyor's chain (66 feet) is the unit in common use in Canada:

1 link	=	7.92 inches
25 links	=	1 rod/5.5 yards
1 chain	=	100 links/66 feet/4 rods (66 feet or 22 yards was the common road allowance)

However, "a chain" can be 66 feet or 100 feet depending on who is doing the survey. I have encountered the 100-foot Ramden's, or engineer's chain, used in surveying land around Fort Cumberland in early Nova Scotia, presumably by British Army engineers.

1 (Engineer's or Ramden's) link = 1 foot
1 (Engineer's or Ramden's) chain = 100 feet

Surveys, of course, lead to land being divided into grants or farms. Our concern is the size or acreage of our ancestor's property. The first table is from a scribbler for school children, the second is equivalents:

Square or Land Measure	
144 square inches	1 square foot
9 square feet	1 square yard
30¼ square yards	1 pole or perch
40 poles	1 rood
4 roods	1 acre
640 acres	1 mile

An "acre," however, can describe different sized areas even in England, and in Scotland, Ireland, and Wales.

Superficial or Surface Area		
1 square foot	=	144 square inches
1 square yard	=	9 square feet
1 rod (square)	=	30¼ square yards
1 pole/perch (square)	=	30¼ square yards
1 rood (square)	=	40 sq. rods /poles = ¼ acre
1 acre	=	4 roods (square)
1 acre	=	10 square chains
1 acre	=	0.4047 hectare

1 acre (English)	=	4,840 square yards
1 acre (Scottish)	=	6,150.4 square yards/ 1.27066 acres
1 acre (Irish)	=	7,840 square yards/ 1.61984 acres

In Wales the *erw* (4,320 square yards), *stang* (3,240 square yards), and *paladr* are all called an acre. Leicestershire, Westmorland, and Cheshire also have their own local value for the acre.

1 square mile	=	640 acres
1 square mile	=	1 section (western Canada)

Measuring France and New France

The measures used in Canada during the French regime can present problems because the same word will often refer to slightly different distances. The French king's foot was longer than the Englishman's foot, so be careful when translating *un pied* as a foot, or *lieue* as league. In France the *grande lieue* or *lieu de mer*, which was standardized in the fifteenth century, has been worked out to be 3.05 British statute miles.[5] The English league equates to 3 miles.

In France a unit of measurement like *arpent* or *toise* could refer to linear measure, superficial or square measure, or even volume, so you must rely on context to determine which is meant. The units explained here are, for the most part, "of Paris," pre-Revolutionary, pre-metric, and somewhat imprecise. Metric and imperial equivalents are given for comparison.[6]

French Linear Measure			
1 pouce	=	27.07mm	= 1.066 inch
1 pied du roi (French king's foot)	=	12 pouces	
1 pied du roi	=	324.839 millimeters	= 12.8 inches
1 aune (also termed: corde, perche, brasse, canne, verge)	=	3 pieds du roi, 7 pouces	= 1.188 metres
1 toise	=	6 pieds du roi	= 1.949 metres
1 tosie	=	6.395 English feet	
1 perche	=	18 pieds du roi/3 toises	
1 arpent	=	180 pieds du roi	
1 arpent	=	191.08 English feet (pieds anglais)	
84 arpent	=	1 league (*lieu*)	= 4.9 kilometres
1 grande lieu	=	3.05 British statute miles	

Superficial or Surface Area

In 1785, a statute of Quebec regulating the surveying profession, stipulated that lands granted *en seigneurie* before 1760 were to continue being described in French measure, but all grants in English tenure were to be surveyed in English measure.

1 arpent	=	36,802 square feet (pieds carrés anglais)		
1 arpent	=	0.845 acre	=	0.342 hectares
1 toise (square)	=	36 pieds carré	=	3.799 metres square	= 40 square feet
1 toise (volume)	=	216 pieds cube	=	7.404 metres cubed

Metric Survey	
The metric surveyor's chain in France had two defined lengths:	
1 chaînon [link]	= can be either 10 centimetres or 20 centimetres[7]
100 chaînons	= 1 chaîne d'arpenteur/ d'arpentage
chaîne decametre	= 10 metres (30.7845 pieds du roi)
chaîne double/decametre	= 20 metres (61.569 pieds du roi)[8]

Other Obsolete Units of Measure

During the first half of this century, tables like these were printed on the back cover of most school exercise books, along with the addition and multiplication tables pupils were expected to memorize. For adults, I have added a few others from the kitchen and the wine merchant as well as some measures found in eighteenth and nineteenth century shipping manifests.

Dry Measure		
1 pint	=	34.68 cubic inches
1 American pint	=	33.60 cubic inches
2 pints	=	1 quart
4 quarts	=	1 gallon
2 gallons	=	1 peck
4 pecks	=	1 bushel
8 bushels	=	1 quarter
36 bushels	=	1 chaldron (chauldron)[9]
Measure of Capacity		
1 pint	=	20 fluid ounces
1 American pint	=	16 fluid ounces
4 gills	=	1 pint
2 pints	=	1 quart
1 British quart	=	40 ounces
1 American quart	=	32 ounces
4 quarts	=	1 gallon
1 British gallon	=	160 fluid ounces
1 American gallon	=	128 fluid ounces
9 gallons	=	1 firkin
36 gallons	=	1 barrel
163 gallons	=	1 hogshead

Kitchen Measures (Capacity)		
4 teaspoons liquid	=	1 tablespoon
2 tablespoons	=	1 ounce
4 tablespoons	=	1 quarter cup
Half cup	=	1 gill
1 cup	=	8 ounces
2 cups	=	1 American pint
4 cups	=	1 American quart

Wine Measure (Capacity)		
1 wine gallon	=	231 cubic inches or 1 American gallon
1 wine barrel	=	30 wine gallons
1 tierce	=	42 wine gallons
1 tierce	=	1 third pipe
2 wine barrels	=	1 hogshead
4 wine barrels	=	1 pipe
1 pipe	=	126 wine gallons
2 pipes	=	1 tun
1 tun	=	252 wine gallons

Kitchen Equivalents		
0.4536 kilogram	=	1 pound
2 cups of butter, solid	=	1 pound
2 cups granulated sugar	=	1 pound
3 cups brown sugar	=	1 pound
1 pint of milk or water	=	1 pound
4 cups pastry/cake flour	=	1 pound
3¾ cups bread flour	=	1 pound

Wine Bottle Sizes		
Bottle	=	750 millilitres/26.4 ounces
Magnum	=	2 bottles
Double magnum	=	4 bottles
Tappit-Hen	=	3 imperial quarts
Jerboam	=	4 bottles
Rebohan	=	6 bottles
Methuselah	=	8 bottles
Salmanazar	=	12 bottles
Balthazar	=	16 bottles
Nebuchadnezzar	=	20 bottles

Bartender's Measures		
1 small jigger	=	1 ounce
1 jigger	=	1½ ounces
1 large jigger	=	2 ounces
1 pony	=	1 ounce
1 liqueur glass	=	1 ounce
1 sherry/port glass	=	2 ounces
1 cocktail glass	=	2 ounces
1 wine glass	=	4 ounces
1 champagne glass	=	5 ounces
1 tumbler	=	8 ounces

Avoirdupois Weight		
16 drams	=	1 ounce
16 ounces	=	1 pound
14 pounds	=	1 stone

25 pounds	=	1 quarter Can.
28 pounds	=	1 quarter U.K.
4 quarters	=	1 hundredweight
1 quintal	=	1 hundredweight U.K.
20 hundredweight	=	1 ton
2,000 pounds Can.	=	1 ton
2,240 pounds U.K.	=	1 ton

Troy Weight		
24 grains	=	1 pennyweight
20 pennyweights	=	1 ounce
12 ounces	=	1 pound

Apothecaries' Weight		
20 grains	=	1 scruple
3 scruples	=	1 dram
8 drams	=	1 ounce
12 ounces	=	1 pound

Cloth Measure		
2¼ inches	=	1 nail
4 nails	=	1 quarter
3 quarters	=	1 Flemish ell
4 quarters	=	1 yard
36 inches	=	1 yard
5 quarters	=	1 English ell
6 quarters	=	1 French ell
37 inches	=	1 Scottish ell

Paper		
24 sheets	=	1 quire
20 quires	=	1 ream

Cubic or Solid Measure		
1,728 inches	=	1 solid foot
27 feet	=	1 solid yard
42 feet	=	1 ton shipping
128 feet	=	1 cord of wood

Units of Trade		
12 (of any item)	=	1 dozen
13 (of any item)	=	1 baker's dozen
12 dozen (144)	=	1 gross
1 cade	=	a barrel or cask
1 cade of red herring	=	500
1 cade of sprats	=	1,000
1 dicker	=	10 hides/skins
1 dicker of gloves	=	10 dozen pairs
1 last of hides	=	20 dickers
1 last	=	a load or cargo, a variable measure but often 4,000 pounds
Quintal, as used for fish	=	112 pounds or 1 British hundredweight
Seroon	=	a form of packaging like a basket or hamper used for tea, raisins, tobacco, without any exact weight

Printers' Measures		
Type size (vertical height) is measured in points		
1 Point	=	.0138 inch
Once each size of type had a name.		
Pearl	=	5 point
Agate	=	5.5 point
14 agate lines	=	1 column inch
Nonpareil	=	6 points
Minion	=	6 points
Brevier	=	8 points
Bourgeois	=	9 points
Long primer	=	10 points
Small pica	=	11 points
Pica	=	12 points
6 picas	=	1 inch
English	=	14 points
Great Primer	=	18 points
An em	=	a blank square space equal to the capital M of whatever type size is being used
An en	=	half an em, or the space equal to the capital N in that font
A thin space	=	a quarter or third of an em

Authorities researchers can consult regarding antique weights and measures:

Zupko, Ronald Edward. *A Dictionary of English Weights and Measures: From Anglo-Saxon Times to the Nineteenth Century.* Madison: University of Wisconsin Press, 1968.

_____. *French Weights and Measures Before the Revolution: A Dictionary of Provincial and Local Units.* Bloomington: University of Indiana Press, 1978.

A useful but less formal source is Thomas J. Glover's *Pocket Ref,* a compilation of facts and data on almost everything, mapping and surveying included, available in Canada from Lee Valley Tools.

Chapter 5

Money

Pennies don't fall from Heaven.
They have to be earned on earth.[1]

Currency

Almost anything you can think of has been used as currency at one time or another, but most money, or mediums of exchange, came in one of two forms:

1. coins or tokens, whose value was originally based on metal content, silver, gold, or copper.

2. printed paper, which was a signed promise to "pay to bearer" in gold or silver.

Information on the variations and details of historical currency, even for a single country, can fill hundreds of pages. Since many people collect old money, both metal and paper, there is a variety of catalogues and guide books listing and illustrating the historical coinage of almost every part of the world. My examples are from British North America.

Coins and Tokens

Dealing with a family estate, I came upon a tea canister half-full of old coins, mostly copper coins and tokens, some large cents, and a few silver sixpence and five-cent pieces. A few were old American cents and a dime. The oldest were a George II 1757 halfpenny, a very worn American *fugio* cent (1787), and a large very worn French coin dated 1792, imprinted with the head of what might have been Louis XVI. It was the halfpenny tokens that I found most fascinating. One, dated 1813, bore the head of Field Marshal Wellington, crowned with a laurel wreath. Two others had a full-rigged ship flying a Union Jack on one side, while the other read SHIPS COLONIES & COMMERCE; another dated 1812 had a slogan TRADE & NAVIGATION surrounding a seated figure of Britannia, and on the other side the statement PURE COPPER PREFERABLE TO PAPER.

That tiny treasure trove reminds us that, until the mid-nineteenth century, the money that circulated in North American was a very mixed lot. In every colony there was an ongoing shortage of actual coins (*specie*) of both high and low value. Small denominations were in especially short supply, and settlers welcomed any medium of exchange, so the coins in circulation came from all over the world.

In New France the legal silver *écu*, as well as the illicit Spanish silver dollar were both in use, together with "card money," an informal but officially signed and sealed form of paper money. Five weeks after the fall of Quebec in 1759, the French government repudiated the obligations represented by the card money, eventually redeeming most of it at about 25 percent of face value. This gave paper money a bad reputation; silver or gold was the preferred form of payment.

Sterling

In Chaucer's England, the silver penny was the standard monetary unit. Two hundred and forty pennies constituted a pound — literally a pound of silver — and the British monetary system evolved from this base of sterling silver (92½ percent purity).

As a result, in British colonies you will find tax assessments and other official valuations given in pounds, shillings, and pence, although little sterling currency was actually in use.

To refresh your memory, here is a table that predates sterling's decimal conversion. The exchange rates in the right-hand column suggest the scribbler it was taken from predates the Second World War.

Pre 1971 English Money Table			
4 Farthings	= 1 Penny (d.)	A Florin is 2s.	= 45¢
12 Pence	= 1 Shilling (s.)	A Half Crown is 2s. 6d.	= 60¢
20 Shillings	= 1 Pound (£)	A Sovereign is 20s.	= $4.86

Pre-decimal sterling is typically written as: £2-13-7 or £2/13/7 (2 pounds, 13 shillings, 7 pence), 14s 4d or 14/4 (14 shillings, 4 pence).

The sovereign and half-sovereign were gold coins. The sovereign coin was taken out of circulation in 1932. "Quid" is slang for a sovereign, or a 1 pound note.

The crown (5 shillings), half crown, florin (2 shillings), shilling, sixpence, and threepence were silver coins. "Bob" is slang for a shilling, "tanner" for sixpence, "groat" for fourpence (coined from 1351 to 1662, and 1836 to 1856). The half crown was removed from circulation in 1970.

The penny (pluralized as pence), halfpenny, and farthing were made of copper until 1860, then bronze. "Copper" is slang for a penny (and for a large cent in Canada[2]). The farthing coin was withdrawn in 1961. The halfpenny (ha'penny) bronze coin was withdrawn 1984.

Decimal conversion took place between 1968 and 15 February 1971. Today there are 100 new pence in a pound, with a penny and two penny coins, 5, 10, 20, and 50 pence coins, and one and two pound coins, all smaller and lighter in weight than formerly, but of different shapes and easily distinguishable sizes.

Silver Dollars

In the Americas, by the seventeenth century, most trade was actually conducted in dollars, which were "pieces-of-eight," the milled Spanish silver coin worth 8 *reals*. *Dollar* is word derived from *thaler*, a German silver coin that once circulated widely in Europe, but the term dollar became attached to the silver coin used throughout the Americas. The value of the dollar could vary.

"Will you be paying in Halifax currency or York?"

In 1708, Britain set the value of the Spanish dollar at 6 shillings. However, later in the century in Massachusetts and Nova Scotia, the Spanish silver dollar was rated at 5 shillings, but in the New York colony it was rated at 7 shillings 6 pence, and a little later at 8 shillings. That is why we often encounter different "monies of account" used by merchants from these colonies: Halifax currency used the 5 shilling rating, while York currency used the New York valuation. In North America, documents or deeds of sale may refer to "Halifax currency" or "York currency," or possibly "provincial currency."

Monies of account are currencies for which no coinage or bills existed, the values having been fixed by government decree. A curious money of account was the Hudson's Bay Company's "made beaver," equal to the value of a prime male beaver pelt. As a commodity, the value varied, but the Company issued a token of this value in 1854.

- In 1764, the British administration passed an ordinance establishing official ratings in British currency of all coins circulating. The Spanish dollar remained at a value of 6 shillings. but during the American Revolution this was reduced to 5 shillings, making Halifax currency the standard. However, York currency valuation was still widely used in Montreal and Upper Canada.

- In 1785, the newly formed United States formally retained the dollar as the standard unit of currency with decimal subdivisions: mill, cent, and dollar. The mill is a money of account only, and there are a thousand in a dollar. Although the first true American dollar was minted in 1794, Spanish dollars continued in use and remained legal tender until 1857.

The adoption of decimal coinage by the United States caused much of its older silver to come to Canada where it was over-valued, but welcome because of the ongoing shortage of coins. Britain had granted most of the colonies in British North America permission to coin copper, so provincial pennies and ha'pennies circulated with the many copper tokens issued by banks, merchants, and manufacturers. The official shift from sterling to decimal (dollar) was gradual. (See the Chronology on page 84.)

Gold Coinage

In Britain and its colonies, gold coinage was a secondary part of the monetary system, since it it was based on sterling silver. Gold coins, however, had always been around in one form or another. A few you may encounter are:

> **Moidore:** Pirate treasure, consisting of gold *moidores*, is not entirely romantic fiction. Moidores were Portuguese *moeda d'ouro* (money of gold), coined from 1640 to 1732, with a sterling value of 13 shillings 5½ pence. The double moidore was rated at 27 shillings, and circulated long after it

ceased to be struck. In the early eighteenth century, it could be found in Europe, particularly widely in Ireland as well in the West Indies, especially Barbados.

Doubloon: An obsolete Spanish gold coin originally worth 16 silver dollars, the doubloon's value was later reduced to five.

Guinea: First coined in Britain in 1663, the Guinea was made from gold brought from the Guinea coast of West Africa. It was last issued in 1813, but until decimalization in 1971, It remained a money of account worth 21 shillings, and was widely used for calculating professional fees and pricing luxury goods. A "spade guinea" had a spade-shaped shield on one side and the monarch's head on the other.

Sovereign: An English gold coin worth 20 shillings, or one pound, it was first struck during the reign of Henry VII (1489), but was chosen as the standard unit of currency (£1) when a gold standard was established in 1816. The first issue was circulated in 1817, along with a half-sovereign.

Other British: Two-pound gold pieces were issued during the reigns of George IV, Victoria, and Edward VII, as well as 5-pound pieces during the reigns of Victoria and Edward VII.[3]

On and off the Gold Standard

Sterling had started to slip off the silver standard as early as 1771, when the master of the mint, Sir Isaac Newton, undervalued sterling and the Royal Mint coined gold as a supplement. By 1774, the debased silver currency was not legal tender for debts over 25 pounds. British currency remained bimetal until after the Napoleonic Wars. The Coinage Act of 1816 formally linked the value of the pound to 113 grains of pure gold.

In Canada, the adoption of both decimal coinage and a gold standard vacillated from 1841 to 1851 when decimal coinage (and a gold standard) were finally adopted. It took two more years to get the formal acts through Parliament and confirmed by the British government. Canada continued on the gold standard until 1914, then went back and forth, following as the rest of the world also switched on and off, off and on, providing economic historians material for countless studies.

Having — or not having — a fixed price for gold probably meant little to our ancestors, except as it affected the price of a wedding ring. I vaguely remember when it was $35.00 an ounce and even a gold chain was affordable.

Paper Money

> BANK-NOTES. "For our present purpose we include in this description all paper substitutes for metallic currency whether issued by banks, governments or other financial institutes."[4]

Banknote, a banker's promissory note, esp. from a central bank, payable to the bearer on demand, and serving as money.[5]

In British North America, the main reason for the establishment of banks was to provide a reliable paper money issue. In 1792, a few 5 shilling notes were issued by the Canadian Banking Company, but there is no proof that this institution actually functioned as a commercial bank.

During the war of 1812, Sir Isaac Brock arranged a printing of army bills (denominated in Halifax dollars), and in spite of many merchant's suspicions (those merchants issued the token recommending *pure copper*), these bills were fully redeemable at the end of the war in silver or gold.

Over the next half-century, colonial and provincial governments gradually issued notes, as did chartered banks and quite a few non-existent ghost banks. There were also merchant's notes, scrip, and bons, in almost as many varieties as there were coins and tokens.

Dominion of Canada Obsolete Coinage

The large cent, the small silver five-cent "bit," and the silver fifty cent coin have by now all disappeared from our pockets and into coin collections, as has the small paper bill, the 25 cent "shin plaster."

Large cent (25.40 millimetres in diameter), bronze	
Queen Victoria	1876–1901
King Edward VII	1901–1910
King George V	1910–1920

The first small cent (19.05 millimetres in diameter) was issued in 1920

Small 5 cent silver coin (15.49 millimetres in diameter)		
Queen Victoria	1858–1901	silver (.925)
King Edward VII	1902–1910	silver (.925)
King George V	1910–1919	silver (.925)
	1920–1921	silver (.800)

Over two-and-a-half million of the 1921 coins were struck before the decision to use a larger nickel coin for this denomination. All the coins were melted down, except about 100 that had been sold as part of a complete set by the mint.

50 cent silver coin (29.72 millimetres in diameter)		
Queen Victoria	1870–1901	silver (.925)
King Edward VII	1902–1910	silver (.925)
King George V	1911–1919	silver (.925)
	1920–1936	silver (.800)
King George VI	1937–1952	silver (.800)
Elizabeth II	1953–1967	silver (.800)
	1968–1974	nickel (27.13)

Canadian Finance — a Chronology

1853 The Provinces of Canada Currency Act legalized transactions in decimal currency for the first time. Gold coin was made unlimited legal tender.

1858 On 1 January, an act came into force requiring that the Province of Canada's accounts be kept in dollars and cents. The first shipment of Canadian coins was received from the British mint by mid-year.

1 July, first Canadian coins introduced: 1¢, 5¢, 10¢, and 20¢.

1867 Following Confederation, Parliament took over control of currency.

1871 The Uniform Currency Act repealed provincial currency acts wherever they were in conflict with federal control. Under this act, banks continued to issue currency, but the Dominion of Canada notes of 25¢, $1.00, and $2.00 also appeared.

1900 First Credit Union in North America founded at Levis, Quebec, by Alphonse Desjardins.

1914 The Finance Act takes Canada off the gold standard during the war.

1917 Federal income tax is introduced as a "temporary wartime measure."

1920 Large (25.40 millimetres in diameter) one cent coins are discontinued.

1923 2 July, last issue of Dominion of Canada 25¢ notes ("shinplasters"). Over five million of these notes were in circulation in 1929.

1926 Canada returns to gold standard.

1929 Canada abandons gold standard, dollar allowed to float.

1934 Bank of Canada is created to regulate currency and credit and given sole permission to issue paper currency. Chartered bank notes were withdrawn over the next 15 years.

1935 Canada's first silver dollar is minted.

1940 Canada introduces Unemployment Insurance.

1945 Canada introduces the Family Allowance (Baby Bonus).

1957 The Canadian dollar rises to $1.06 U.S.

1962 The Canadian dollar is pegged to U.S. dollar at 92.5¢ U.S., and remains there until 1970.
The 25¢ coin is changed from .800 silver to .500 silver, then discontinued, replaced by nickel coin.

1965 Canadian–U.S. Automotive Products Agreement is reached.
The Canada Pension Plan and the Quebec Pension Plan are introduced.

1966 Federal Medical Care Act

1968 The Chargex, now known as Visa, credit card is introduced in Canada.

1972 Canada introduces the Capital Gains Tax.

1974 The 50¢ coin is discontinued.

1976 Eaton's halts catalogue sales.

1979 Canada's first gold bullion coin goes on sale.

1981 The Bank of Canada lending rate rises to 21 percent, and the prime lending rate rises to 22.75 percent.

1982 Canada is hit by a severe recession, which lasts over 18 months.

1987 The $1.00 coin (loonie) is introduced, and no further dollar bills are issued.

1990 The Goods and Service Tax (GST) is introduced.

1995 The $2.00 coin (toonie) is introduced, and no further $2 bills are issued.

Useful Published Sources

Money and Exchange in Canada to 1900 by Alan McCullough (Toronto: Dundurn Press, 1984) is the definitive source on money, with many tables of official ratings and equivalent values over the years.

The Canadian Encyclopedia, currency entry explains the whole tangled web in some detail and can be found online, *http://thecanadianencyclopedia.com/*, or in print by Edmonton: Hurtig, 1985.

The Story of Canada's Currency, printed for the Bank of Canada (Ottawa: 1981, third edition), gives a simpler, but more entertaining account, in its brief 38 pages.

In Canada East, accounts were still kept in pounds, shillings, and pence, but James Douglas was attempting to understand the American decimal system, if somewhat imperfectly.

Chapter 6

The Value of Money: It's Not What It Used to Be

What Will a Penny Buy?

Coins and notes are all very interesting, but what really matters is what they are worth: what could my ancestor buy with a penny? Some of the earliest written records document what people were paid and what things cost. There are countless books, by historians and economists, comparing the purchasing power of monies at different times. Regardless of when or where an individual lived, the basic question we must try to answer is: how long did someone have to work to earn enough to pay for the necessities of life?

The process is simple, though not necessarily easy. Find a list of what various workers were paid and lists of prices for food, clothing, and shelter. For Canadian statistics between 1868 and 1925, the Auditor General's report in the *Sessional Papers of the Dominion of Canada*[1] provides lists of wages and salaries paid to all government employees, from top executives and their secretaries down to postal clerks and apprentices in the railway shop. Local newspaper advertisements or Eaton's mail-order catalogues provide costs.

An Example: One of my grandfathers was a skilled craftsman, a boilermaker. He worked for the Intercolonial Railway (ICR) in the Moncton Locomotive Shop. In 1907–08 he worked 2,546 hours and was paid almost the top hourly wage — 27¢ an hour — earning $687.42 between April and March (the Federal fiscal year). My other grandfather was a federal fisheries inspector, and he received an annual salary of $1,300. The general manager of the ICR (D. Pottinger) had an annual salary of $6,000, his chief clerk earned $1,800. Some 30 years earlier (1878) D. Pottinger had been general storekeeper for the ICR Stores Department, earning $1,800. This was before there were income tax and other payroll deductions.[2]

At Eaton's from 1907 to 1910, blue denim overalls with bib and strap cost 50¢, and a man's double-breasted suit cost from $5.50 to $16.50. A pound of tea or coffee could be bought for 35¢, a 50-pound tub of pure leaf lard cost $6.00, a three-pound tin of molasses was 18¢, women's "good cotton" drawers and corset covers ranged from

19¢ to 85¢, and a large bracket oil lamp cost 48¢. A top quality buggy cost $65.00. Again, this is an era before sales taxes.[3]

The boilermaker had to work for almost two hours to earn enough to buy his blue denim overalls, if that was what he wore to work. The fisheries inspector would pay over half-a-month's salary for the new buggy (horse not included) he needed to get from wharf to wharf. Mr. Pottinger, however, could easily afford the latest toy, a Columbia Sterling talking machine at $50.00, which played the new flat disc records instead of the older cylinders.

Heed this warning: make sure that the wages and prices you find derive from the same country at the same point in time. Inflation is only one of the factors that can radically changed the value of labour and money. History offers many examples.

Chaucer's Penny

The poet Geoffrey Chaucer lived from 1345 to 1400, and in the year of his birth a penny could buy far more in both goods and services than when he died. Bubonic plague was sweeping across Europe, and reached England in 1349. In 1348, the population of England was between six and seven million people: the Black Death killed between one third and one half of them in a matter of months.[4] There was a sudden shift of wealth and power. Survivors inherited unexpected land or money only to find that hired help, both skilled and unskilled, was in very short supply. Suddenly everyone's labour was worth far more than it had been before the plague years.

- Before 1348, a ploughman was paid around 8 pence per acre. After the plague, it cost from a shilling to one-and-sixpence for the same job. By 1350, ordinary farm labourers, like threshers, were paid 2 to 3 pence per day, the more skilled mower as much as 5 pence a day. In 1361, the clerk of the works at Sheppy Castle was paid 1 shilling a day, the Earl of Arundel's pay as admiral of the fleet in 1385 was 6 shillings 8 pence daily.

- Prices also rose. Salt went up from 5¼ to 9½ pence a bushel, the cost of ploughshares from 9 shillings 9 pence to 19 shillings 1¾ pence, a dozen ells of linen from 4 shillings 1¾ pence to 8 shillings 4½ pence. The clerk at Sheppy castle would have to work close to two weeks (12 days) to earn the price of a cow, which was around 11 shillings 10¾ pence. A cart-horse cost 23 shillings 9½ pence — about twice the price of the cow.[5]

- With labour both scarce and expensive, many landowners turned to raising sheep instead of grain. More land was enclosed as pasture, and better fed sheep produced more and better wool. The wool trade and

cloth weaving were already a vital part of
the economy of Britain. At least four of
Chaucer's Canterbury Pilgrims were in
the cloth trade, the best known his "Wif
of biside Bathe" whose skill "passed hem of
Ypres and of Gaunt."

I realize that, except for exalted families and a few
lucky genealogists, not many of us can trace their ancestry
back to the fourteenth century. Even so, those values and
prices, which I found for my 1956 thesis, teaches us several lessons: inflation is not a new phenomenon and if, for
any reason (plague, war, natural disaster), labour becomes
scarce, wages will rise and with them the price of the necessities of life.

What Is a Necessity?

Another question researchers must take into consideration
is: what lifestyle did your ancestors aspired to?

Until well into the nineteenth century, almost everything was made by hand. In England, skilled workmen
were paid reasonably well, meaning that, in terms of
"working days needed to buy," products were expensive.
Even so, well-paid craftsmen could live a better life in town
than an agricultural labourer on some nobleman's estate.
Farm hand, master craftsman, aristocrat, each had a different standard of living and different ideas of what was a
necessity.

Lucky time travellers often get back to the mid-eighteenth,
or early nineteenth century, so let's have a look.

From Dr. Johnson's Penny to Madame d'Arblay's Pound

Dr. Samuel Johnson (1709–1784), the famous English writer, had a protégé: the novelist Fanny Burney (1752–1840). Their lives bracket decades of wars and revolutions. There was inflation, and the cost of living fluctuated, sometimes wildly as you can see if you go to the Bank of England website where a graph allows you calculate the difference in the value of a pound for any two years between 1750 and 2008. (Be sure to read the "calculator caveats.")

Our impression of the eighteenth and early nineteenth century is coloured by novels, as well as period films and television shows. Most are set in stately homes or picturesque villages, with an occasional sortie into a squalid garret. Some give quite an accurate picture of how people lived. But what kind of income was required to live in a stately home, or at a respectable address in London, in a cottage or a garret? The difference is enormous.

With industry dependent on coal, it was advantageous if your income was somehow tied to coal production. One family had that advantage: Charles II, to support his illegitimate son the Duke of Richmond (1672–1723), gave him and his heirs a royalty of 12 pence per cauldron on coal dues (taxes) at Newcastle. "At the beginning of the eighteenth century the coal dues already produced five thousand pounds a year, a sum on which an aristocrat, his family, servants and horses could live in style." By the 1790s, the amount had shot up to over twenty thousand pounds annually, prompting Tom Paine, a radical, to remark: "the Duke of Richmond takes away as much for himself as would maintain two thousand poor and aged persons."[6]

In the 1790s, to finance the wars with France, the British government initiated a variety of taxes on luxuries, such as coaches, men servants, hair powder, and windows. Even a tenant farmer in Scotland paid a tax on his windows, work horses, and dogs. The taxes continued well after the Napoleonic wars, that being the nature of taxes.

That amounted to 10 pounds a year for each poor or aged person. Was 10 pounds sufficient to live on in 1790, or is that political hyperbole? What *did* it cost to live back then? In 1763, James Boswell consulted Dr. Johnson on the subject. A very poor Samuel Johnson, who came to London in 1737,

> … was told by a very clever man who understood perfectly the common affairs of life that £30 a year was enough to make a man live without being contemptible; that is to say you might always be clean. He allowed £10 for clothes and linen. He said you might live in a garret at eighteen-pence a week [£3/18 a year], as few people would inquire where you lodge; and if they do, it is easy to say, "Sir, I am to be found at such a place." For spending threepence in a coffee house, you may be for hours in very

good company. You may dine for sixpence
[£9/2/6 a year], you may breakfast on bread
and milk, and you may want supper.[7]

The young, single Boswell had an allowance from his
father of £200 a year and drew up a budget allowing £50
for lodging, another £50 for clothes, £10 for stockings and
shoes, and £6 for wax candles, which had "a finer light"
and could be locked up without offence. He planned to
breakfast in his rooms. His total came to £164 leaving the
remaining £36 for coach hire, diversions, and the tavern,
"which I will find a very slight allowance."[8]

The Upper Aristocracy

Janet Gleeson, in her meticulously documented biography
of Lady Harriet Spencer, explains the 1780 marriage settlement between two titled families:

> Lord Bessborough ... had left the family
> heavily indebted. He could offer only
> £2,000 a year for the couple [Lord and
> Lady Duncannon] to live on and £400
> a year pin money (the only money an
> aristocratic woman had to spend as
> she wished — thus her only financial
> independence) for Harriet.... this was
> less than a tenth of what Georgiana [her
> sister, the Duchess of Devonshire] had to
> live on and far less than Harriet had been
> used to enjoying.[9]

By 1821, John George Lambton (later Lord Durham of Canada's Durham Report) thought that £40,000 a year was a moderate income, "such a one as a man might jog on with." He was probably the richest commoner in England, and he may have been making a joke. Remember, however, that these families were the top of the British ruling class. Their standard of living was far above most members of the general population, even the gentry, who were often related to them through cadet lines (families of younger sons) or marriage.[10]

The Gentry

Jane Austen was a member of this gentry. When her father died, most of his income as a clergyman died with him. Mrs. Austen "was suddenly reduced to the status of a widow faced with the dreary prospect of having to support herself and two grown-up daughters on an income of £210 per year." Her sons rallied around her, increasing her annual income to about £460. "In 1805 this meant she was, if not rich, relatively comfortable, able to keep at least one live-in servant, with enough free money for her and each of her daughters to afford an occasional visit to their friends and relations."[11]

Let's stay with Jane Austen; she was forthright in discussing the importance of money and fully understood the subtle social differences that separated the upper class and the emerging middle class. In *Pride and Prejudice*, Mr. Bingley's £5,000 a year was considered a handsome income, and Mr. Darcy's £10,000 munificent. Darcy's family were long-established land-owners and Darcy himself was the nephew of an Earl. However, the Bingley sisters "… were of a respectable family in the north of England, a circumstance more deeply impressed on their memories than that their brother's fortune and their own had been acquired by trade."[12]

Mr. Bingley's sisters "were very anxious for his having an estate of his own" so he would hopefully be considered a member of the landed gentry, "though he was now established only as a tenant."

In *Sense and Sensibility*, the Dashwood family's finances are set forth in great detail. Jane Austen assumes a 5 percent return on capital, so the widowed Mrs. Dashwood and her three daughters would have £500 per year; slightly better than the widow Austen and her two daughters had.

- In both novels, Mr Bennet's and Colonel Brandon's incomes of £2,000 a year are considered more than adequate to maintain a wife and family in good county society.

- Colonel Brandon, apologizes because the living he can offer Edward Ferrars is only a small rectory with an income of about £200, which would keep him "comfortable as a bachelor, but it cannot enable him to marry."[13]

- All Edward had, in addition to the small income, was £2,000 from his mother when she disinherited him; his eventual bride, Eleanor Dashwood, had only £1,000 marriage portion. £3,000 would add at most £150 a year.

Single Women

Fanny Burney wrote novels a generation before Jane Austen. Fanny Burney's second, *Cecilia*, can be seen as a precursor to *Pride and Prejudice*. Her writing brought a degree of celebrity, but no regular income. From 1786 to 1791, Fanny Burney served Queen Charlotte as a second keeper of the robes, a prestigious but tedious job at Court that she did not much care for.

- Fanny Burney's salary was £200 a year, room and board in drafty palaces included. She probably had to spend most of it on her wardrobe, since there were strict rules about dress at court. When poor health allowed her to escape, the Queen granted her an annual pension of £100, paid quarterly.

- Note that from 1799 until 24 May 1816 this pension had £10 (10 percent) income tax deducted (£2/10 per quarter).

- £100 (or, more realistically, £90) was considered a generous sum, and quite adequate for an unmarried woman who would typically be living with her family and not expected to maintain a household with servants or a carriage and horses of her own. Jane Austen's heroines had at most, half of that.

- Half a century later, in 1847, Jane Eyre was to be paid £30 a year (plus room and board) as a governess. When an uncle leaves her £20,000, she insists on sharing it equally with her cousins so that "St.John, Diana, Mary, and I, each became possessed of a competency."[14] The interest on £5,000 would have been between £150 and £250 per year, depending on which government funds they invested in.

When she made her will in 1839, Fanny Burney, la Comtesse Veuve Piochard d'Arblay, was still receiving her royal pension of £100 a year. Fortunately she had other income from investments in both English and French funds. Madame d'Arblay was able to live modestly, with one servant, in London in rooms, first at 11 Bolton Street, then No.1 Half-Moon Street, on a yearly income that in 1839 she stated was about £431/5/4 "subject to some little variation from the change in the rate of exchange."[15] In her will, Fanny left a lifetime bequest of £200 per annum to her half-sister Sarah Harriet Burney, double what her own royal pension had been in 1791.

James Boswell's allowance of £200 in the 1760s could buy almost twice what Jane Eyre and Sarah Harriet's £200 did in the 1840s. At the beginning of the nineteenth century, Mr. Bingley's £5,000 couldn't provide the lifestyle that the same sum had allowed the Duke of Richmond a century earlier. However, the thing to watch out for here is not inflation, but the fact that one person could live respectably on £200. The bulk of the population probably survived on under £20. Yet some couldn't manage with 10 times that amount.

- When judging the past, it is important to recognize what lifestyle an individual was expected to maintain before evaluating their income. This was a society where a few titled families were vastly rich (rather like today's star athletes, entertainers, and merchant bankers), a lot of the population was truly poor, and in between was a growing middle class that aspired to the lifestyle of the long established land-owning gentry.

- The great houses, where the aristocracy once lived, took an army of servants to maintain. They had a large payroll to be met every year. The upkeep and repairs would have been a considerable drain as well.

- If £400 was totally inadequate "pin money" for the first Earl Spenser's daughter, the soon to be Countess of Bessborough, 50 years later it was enough for Madame d'Arblay to live on respectably in London.

Both women became countesses but there is one difference: as Fanny Burney more than once explained, she only used the title when claiming her husband's pension:

> ... our limited income, & the decided English destiny of Alex [their son], determined our dropping the Title bestowed by the French King at Ghent, — but as it is entered at the *War Office*, & at the *Bank*, I can, Now, make known no right but by taking it up.[16]

* * *

I have never borne my Title, because I have
had no Fortune to meet it; & because my
son relinquished his hereditary claims of
succession ... on becoming a Clergyman of
the Church of England.[17]

The Late Nineteenth Century

As detailed in Chapter 1, technological revolutions produced
a new and very different world. By 1850, for instance, steam
power had replaced a lot of men and a great many horses.
However, in doing so it created new jobs and new products.
Our ancestors transitioned from a made-by-hand, medieval
or seventeenth-century world into the twentieth century.

But take care: it happened at different speeds and at different times in different places. One quick way to estimate
a date is to ask "When did the railway come through?" As
a network of rails spread around the world, things changed
whenever and wherever trains began to run.

The Twentieth Century

The technologies of the twentieth century are familiar to us.
Many were perfected during the First and Second World
Wars; you cannot escape the after-effects of those wars as
you travel back in time searching for your ancestors:

- The end of a war means unemployment, not
  just for the soldiers and sailors, but for the
  builders of ships, tanks, or aeroplanes, the
  makers of uniforms, boots, saddles, swords,

guns, and cannons. The results can be economic depression, inflation, and civil unrest.

- All of these after-effects of war happened in 1816 and 1819, bringing many unemployed Britons to Canada. By 1946 governments were better at restarting civilian economies, both their own and their enemies. The Marshall Plan (1947–52) helped rebuild much of Western Europe.

- In Canada, many veterans were sent back to school or university, which meant they did not demand instant jobs. Instead, they were allowed "sixty dollars a month tax free,"[18] and young working-class men, and a few women, who had never expected to attend university, earned degrees and entered professions. The social and economic shift was significant for many of that generation — watch out for it.

Inflation Continues

In 1956, I was trying to understand what Chaucer's penny was worth in terms of contemporary dollars. I didn't have a computer or Internet Inflation Calculator, but I had a extensive list of agricultural costs and prices from 1350 to 1400 and I also had in-laws still farming a family farm.

- I consulted my in-laws about agricultural wages, costs, and prices. By comparing produce and livestock prices, as well as farm labour costs we came up with a guesstimate that Can$1.50 would buy about as much grain or unskilled labour as Chaucer's penny did in 1390.

- In 2006, 50 years later, to buy what that Can$1.50 (Chaucer's penny) would in 1956, I would have needed Can$11.42.

- Like Chaucer's penny, the Canadian dollar buys a lot less in 2010 than it did when I was born. The Bank of Canada's website has a section where you can calculate the change in the dollar's value between any years from 1914 to 2009. The value of the 1972 dollar was reduced to 26¢ in twenty years. By 1992, you needed $3.80 to buy what a dollar would in 1972.

When I checked the Bank of England statistics on inflation, their numbers were different as were calculations for the United States, so place matters as well as time.

One More Thing

There is one more thing to consider when evaluating the buying power of money. What Jane Austen could purchase in 1809 and what my grandfathers could buy in 1909 were rarely the same products. Revolutions in manufacturing, transportation, and refrigeration changed what was available; moreover it changed what people thought they needed. In the 80 years between 1929 and 2009, the things I can buy with my steadily devaluing dollar changed almost as much again. That is why "the value of money" has all the permanence of a sandbar that shifts with every tide.

Notable "Bubbles"

1633–37   Holland, Tulip Mania

1719–20   France, Mississippi Bubble

1720   October, Britain's South Sea
              Bubble starts to burst

1840   Britain, Railway bubble

1873   Building and mortgage bubbles
              burst across Europe, precipitates
              depression lasting through 1879

2000   dot.com or Internet bubble bursts

Chapter 7

Travel in the Past

And what is fifty miles of good road?
A little more than half a day's journey.
Yes, I call it a very easy distance.[1]

In the first decade of the twenty-first century, half a day's journey spans a far greater distance than 50 miles (80 kilometres). However, there was a time when that distance took all morning. Now, we have difficulty imagining a time when mankind counted on horsepower or wind power to get from place to place, when water could be the highway and land was often a barrier.

Waterways

Yet, until the mid-twentieth century we sailed to America, Africa, or Asia, and used rivers as highways into the continents. Where rapids, waterfalls, or land blocked the passage of vessels, canals were built.

Canals

Artificial water courses, channels, or canals have been used since ancient times to drain low lying land, for irrigation, and to join bodies of navigable water. Locks were introduced in the late fourteenth or early fifteenth century, allowing canals to link bodies of water of different levels.

Here are a few of many major canal projects:

year	place	name	joins	to
1327	China	Grand Canal	Pei-ho	Yang-tse-Kiang
1681	France	Canal du Midi	Bay of Biscay	Mediterranean
1761	England	Bridgewater	Manchester	Worsley
1825	U.S.	Erie	Hudson River	Lake Erie
1829	Canada	Welland	Lake Ontario	Lake Erie
1832	Canada	Rideau	Ottawa River	Lake Ontario
1845	Germany	Ludwig's Canal	Rhine/Main	Danube
1869	Egypt	Suez	Mediterranean	Red Sea
1895	Germany	Kiel	North Sea	Baltic
1914	Panama	Panama	Atlantic	Pacific
1959	Canada	St. Lawrence Seaway	Atlantic	Great Lakes
1964	Russia	Volga-Baltic	Baltic	Volga (Caspian Sea)
1992	Germany	Main-Danube	North Sea	Black Sea

Canals were the earliest large transportation projects in Canada. The first were built at Coteau-du-Lac in 1783. The Lachine Rapids in the St. Lawrence River above Montreal were bypassed in 1825 by the Lachine Canal, followed by the Welland Canal in 1829, which was built to overcome the obstacle created by the Niagara Falls. The Rideau Canal, whose primary purpose was military, followed.[2]

Wind vs. Steam

Before the steam engine, we relied on wind power to cross the Atlantic, but how long did that take? My grandfather often told me about a difficult return voyage from Cork, Ireland, to New Brunswick on one of his father's sailing-ships, which took 60 days around 1879.

Jane Ellice, wife of Lord Durham's private secretary, gives very precise dates in her diary. Sailing to Quebec with Lord Durham's entourage had taken some five weeks (34 days).

> Tues. 24 April 1838
>
> Sailed in the *Hastings* from Portsmouth.

> Sun. 27 May, 1838
>
> The approach to Quebec however is quite beautiful. We anchored about 12 o'clock. [Lord Durham's party disembarked with considerable ceremony on Tuesday 29 May 1838.]

Remember that the prevailing winds blow from west to east, and crossing from an Atlantic seaboard port to Britain took around three weeks, if all went well. As we read in Jane Ellice's diary, while she hoped for a crossing in three weeks, she was prepared for as much as six weeks on board. The Ellice party's voyage home took a mere 20 days.

The harbour of Quebec City in the days of sail, as engraved by Bouchette.

New York, 26 Nov. 1838

And so we are off! Off to England! ... then went back to our pigeon holes, where we are to pass the next 3, 4, 5, or 6 weeks of our (lately) *too* eventful lives.

Liverpool, Sat. 15 December 1838

And so we poked our way up the Channel, tacking every other foot of the way, & landed at Liverpool about 1 o'clock.[3]

It was about this time, in Halifax, that Samuel Cunard was planning his British and North American Royal Mail Steam Packet Company, now known as the Cunard Line. The Cunard family owned a fleet of sailing vessels engaged in trade with the West Indies, and had been contracted to carry mail by sailing packet between Halifax, Boston, Bermuda, and St. John's, Newfoundland, since 1819.

Samuel Cunard had investigated steam propulsion as early as 1815 in a project to improve ferry service between Halifax and Dartmouth, and was involved with the *Royal William*. Built in Quebec, she was the first steamship to cross the Atlantic from west to east entirely under steam power. On 4 August 1833, she left Quebec City, steamed to Pictou, Nova Scotia, to load coal for the voyage, leaving Pictou on 18 August, arriving 25 days later at Gravesend, down the river from London, on 11 September. The first Cunard Mail Steam Packet arrived in Halifax from Britain on 17 July 1840 in a record time of 14 days, eight hours.

Steam might have been faster, but there were problems. In 1842, Charles Dickens sailed to Boston in one of these new steamships. He found it so smelly, noisy, lurching, and generally uncomfortable that he returned to England by the slower, but gentler, sailing packet. Then, in 1854, Hugh and Andrew Allan established the Montreal Ocean Steamship Company with four steamships running between Montreal and England.

Around the World by Clipper

A major disadvantage of steam for trading voyages was the quantity of fuel that had to be carried, which meant less cargo could be taken aboard. While engineers were developing workable steam ships, other designers were speeding up sailing vessels and perfecting fast and beautiful clipper ships to bring valuable cargo like tea, silk, and wool to market. In 1852, the *Marco Polo*, built in Saint John, New Brunswick, made the trip from Liverpool to Melbourne, Australia, via the Cape of Good Hope, and back around Cape Horn, in five months and 21 days. However, she never matched that time in her subsequent seven trips. The Black-Ball clipper, *Lightning*, captained by James Nicol "Bully" Forbes, the same captain who had driven the *Marco Polo* so hard, made the same trip in five months, eight days, and 21 hours.[4]

Slower than the clippers, East Indiamen were the big, well-appointed and well-armed ships of the Honourable East India Company. They carried passengers and cargo to and from the East for a century and more. The length of their voyages might be closer to that of most vessels, as compared to the clipper's well-publicized races. The HEIC ship the *Marquis of Ely* left the Thames on 16 April 1806, sailed from Portsmouth on 15 May 1806, reached Whampoa, just north of present-day Hong Kong, in China on 10 January 1807, (240 days, or let's say seven months, 25 days out), and returned to the Thames on 27 January 1808, spending over nine months to get home.[5]

For a fuller understanding of what a voyage under sail could be like, Lucille H. Campey's chapter "The Sea crossing" in *Planters, Paupers, and Pioneers* sets out what conditions below deck were like, and explains the economics of the timber over, emigrants back, and transatlantic trade.

Out To India

1835   Lord Auckland, appointed Governor General of India in 1835, set sail with his sisters, the Honourable Emily and Fanny Eden, from Portsmouth on 3 October 1835 on the frigate *Jupiter*. Five months later, on 4 March 1836, the *Jupiter* was in the Hooghly River approaching Calcutta. That was a reasonably fast trip. It could easily take six months or more.[6]

1855/6 When Lord Canning replaced Lord Dalhousie as Governor General of India in 1855, the trip out took only two months. The Canning party spent a few days in Paris to shop, then sailed from Marseilles to Alexandria in early December. After a stop there, they took a train to Cairo for further sight-seeing, then another train to Suez, and sailed from Suez on 12 January 1856 to Bombay (now Mumbai), where they arrived on 29 January.[7]

1898 By the time Lord Curzon of Kedlestone was appointed Viceroy in 1898, the trip took three weeks on the *SS Arabia*. Steamships and the Suez Canal (opened in 1869) made all the difference.[8]

1924 The first flight from England to India was made in 220 hours, just over 9 days.[9]

Don't forget that although new technologies may supplant the old, they do not vanish. Sailing ships survived into the twentieth century for transporting cargo. In 1946, the

435-ton three-masted schooner, *Frederick P. Elkin*, carrying freight, completed a hard 38-day passage from Barbados to Halifax with a cargo of molasses,[10] much as Cunard's schooners had done a century earlier.

Horsepower

Today, riding a horse and driving a coach are hobbies, not essential forms of transportation. When I was researching transportation, I wanted to know how far and how fast someone could travel by horse but it's no longer common knowledge. I turned again to Jane Austen, who wrote in a time when distance was measured in miles and speeds in miles per hour. In *Pride and Prejudice*, Mr. Darcy tells Elizabeth Bennet that a trip of 50 miles over good roads is "little more than half a day's journey."

- If Darcy thought that half a day was about six hours, he was pushing his horses almost as hard as the Royal Mail coaches. These averaged 11 miles per hour, and the working life of those horses was only about four years.[11] Fifty miles, covered at 10 miles per hour, would have required at least one change of horses, and probably more. Darcy, like his aunt Lady Catherine de Bourgh, must have been travelling "post," that is renting fresh horses to pull the coach for each stage of the journey. On a well-travelled "good road" this service would be readily available to those who could afford it. Using your own horses would take considerably longer.

- In *Northanger Abbey*, General Tilney's party broke the 30-mile journey between Bath and the abbey with a two-hour bait (an essential stop for the horses to be watered, fed, and rested) at the halfway point. We are told the trip got underway soon after 10 in the morning and ended about 4:30. The General's chaise-and-four with liveried postilions and outriders was slower than Henry Tilney's curricle, but set the pace at just over six-and-a-half miles per hour.

- Not all roads were good. In *Persuasion*, an excursion to Lyme, "only seventeen miles from Uppercross," is spread over two days, in part because of Mr. Musgrove's reluctance to have his horses on the road for seven hours in a single day, the time "the nature of the country required, for going and returning."[12] So 34 miles, there and back, averages out to a speed of just under five miles an hour.

Jane Austen was amused by young men's preoccupation with the speed and elegance of their gigs, curricles, and horses. Like today's sports cars, good horses and smart carriages were costly, both to buy and maintain. In *Northanger Abbey*, John Thorpe claimed his horse travelled 25 miles in two-and-a-half hours, or at a speed of 10 miles per hour. James Morland's more realistic estimate of 23 miles in three-and-a-half hours suggests that six-and-a-half or seven miles per hour was closer to the truth for a light vehicle pulled by a single horse.

Twenty-five to 30 miles appears to be about the maximum distance a horse could be expected to travel in a day at a speed of five to six miles per hour — but not every day. That is also about the average distance and speed we might expect for someone on horseback.

Steam Power and Railways

Travel changed radically and rapidly with the advent of steam power. Developed in the last quarter of the eighteenth century, steam engines became the nineteenth century's toy for grown-up boys:

1804 Richard Trevithic (1771–1833) builds the first steam rail locomotive at a colliery in South Wales.

1807 Robert Fulton (1765–1815) launches a steam-powered vessel (*Clermont*) that travels almost 150 miles to Albany in 32 hours.

1814 Fulton and the U.S. government builds the first steam warship, *Fulton the First*.

1816 The first steamship travels on the Rhine, the British *Defiance*. Steamships could sail upriver and did not need to stay close to the bank and tow-path.

1817 The second steamship on the Rhine, the British *Caledonia*, piloted by Captain James Watt Jr., son of the inventor.

1825 27 September, Stephenson's engine *Locomotion* hauls the first steam train on a public railway from Stildon to Stockton Quay.[13]

1829 6–14 October, Rainhill Trials[14]

1830 15 September, Liverpool and Manchester Railway opens. It is the "first passenger railway with mechanical traction, up and down roads, proper stations, timetables and signaling of a sort."[15]

Much railway history is written by men in love with locomotives who go on interminably about minute changes in steam traction, while exact information on when lines were finished and actual trains started to carry passengers can be hard to find. Part of the problem is that building railways was a highly speculative operation, many proposals were just "pie in the sky" ideas, and railway bubbles frequently burst.

- Look for passenger trains after 1830. The early railways in Britain, Europe, the eastern coast of the United States, and other long-settled regions linked important commercial centres. For instance, the Liverpool and Manchester line led to other inter-city links: London to Birmingham, London to Southampton, London to Bristol, and Edinburgh to Glasgow.

- The success of these lines in England led to the great "Railway Mania" of the mid-1840s. A few speculators became very wealthy, but many others were ruined, along with the usual widows, orphans, and optimists.

- In much of Europe, where state-established railway systems developed, fewer competitive lines were built. In the U.S. in 1830, the first short section of a line from Charleston, South Carolina, to Hamburg (across the river from Augusta, Georgia) opened. When completed in 1833, the 136 miles (219 kilometres) of track was the longest railroad in the world. Note that Americans call them railroads, not railways.

Canal lock and railway bridge at Ste. Anne's, at the west end of the Island of Montreal. Steam was now what drove both trains and boats. From Picturesque Canada.

Portage Lines

Where money flowed less freely, early portage lines were built to serve the same purpose as a canal: to create a linked transportation system from one body of navigable water to another. These portage lines were actually the beginnings of railways in British North America. For example, the

Intercolonial Railway, which would eventually join the Maritimes to the Canadas, had its start as a portage line linking the Gulf of St. Lawrence at Shediac Bay (Point du Chêne) to the Bay of Fundy at Moncton.

1832 Charter is granted to the Champlain and St. Lawrence Railroad Company.

1836 21 July, the first railway train in Canada pulls two coaches from La Prairie, on the St. Lawrence opposite Montreal, to St. Johns on the Richelieu River, with an average speed of 14.5 miles per hour. This provided a direct link to the water route to New York City and the Atlantic.

1853 18 June, Grand Trunk Railway service, between Montreal and Portland, Maine, begins.

1856 27 October, the Grand Trunk Railway between Montreal and Toronto opens.

1859 On 17 December, in Montreal, the first passenger train crosses the Victoria Bridge (opened on 12 December).

In previously undeveloped regions, a different pattern prevailed. Where governments, or the Crown, owned the land, they saw railways as a way to open and exploit their holdings; settlements and cities followed the rails.

In Canada, the last spike of the Canadian Pacific Railway was driven at on 7 November 1885. On 26 June 1886, the first trans-continental train left Montreal for

Port Moody. There was no Atlantic to Pacific service in the United States, and passengers had to transfer in Chicago.

India had its first railway and telegraph in 1853. Railways came to Chili in 1851, Brazil in 1854, and Argentina in 1857. By 1870, the basic railway systems in Britain, Europe, and the eastern United States were built and running, though branch lines would continue being built well into the twentieth century. Speeds increased from 15 miles per hour to over 50. No horse-drawn vehicle could compete, though they were still needed to take passengers and their luggage to and from the railway stations.

- Railways were how most people moved around rural Canada from the 1850s to the 1950s. People could work quite far from home and commute by train, daily or on weekends. They met and married people from other townships or counties, and might settle down in a growing town.

- Railway lines were once marked on every road map, but many have since vanished. Many libraries now have collections of railway ephemera, which may include maps and timetables. Do not overlook the information such documents contain when tracking down migrant ancestors.

The Horseless Carriage

Rather the way steam supplanted horse, wind, and muscle power over the course of the nineteenth century, electricity and gasoline power supplanted steam over the course of the twentieth.

Experimental steam-driven coaches were terrifying pedestrians as early as 1784, and by 1822, a variety of these were rattling happily along the smooth macadamized roads in Britain, reaching their heyday around 1840. Steam cars continued to be built and sold well into the twentieth century.

1885 Gottlieb Daimler (1834–1900) built one of the earliest roadworthy motor cars with a high-speed internal-combustion engine.

1893 Henry Ford (1863–1947) produced his first gasoline-driven car.

1903 Founding of Ford Motor Company.

1905 Automobile Association (Britain) is founded.

1907 Michelin, a tire company, issued the first road map.

1908 The Ford Model T is introduced. Over 15 million built to 1927.
General Motors founded by William Crapo Durant.

1914 Greyhound Bus Lines started in Hibbing, Minnesota, and incorporated as "Greyhound Corporation" in 1929, the same year Greyhound Canada was founded in Alberta.[16]

Thus, we entered the "Age of Oil, the Automobile and Mass Production," with the First World War waiting in the wings. Also waiting was the flying machine.

By 1934, motor-vehicle registration in Canada increased from 89,944 in 1915 to 728,005 in 1925, and to 1,114,503 in 1932. The latter figure gives an average of one motor vehicle to every 9.4 persons. The United States, New Zealand, and Hawaii were the only places with a greater number per capita, and the United States, France, and the United Kingdom were the only countries having a greater number of motor vehicles registered.[17]

Further information on how Canada's transportation systems developed can be found in the *Historical Atlas of Canada, Vol.II*, Plate 25 "Emergence of a Transportation System, 1837–1852," Plate 26 "The Railway Age, 1834–1891," Plate 27 "Linking Canada, 1867–1891," which has two maps showing the number of days to travel from Ottawa in 1867 and 1891; *Vol.III*, Plate 53 "The Growth of Road and Air Transport."[18]

Airborne at Last

People have always dreamed of flying. There are the Greek tale of Daedalus and Icarus, accounts of their medieval imitators (who also crashed to earth), and Leonardo da Vinci's drawings of flying machines that still intrigue scholars. A small hot-air balloon was demonstrated in Lisbon in 1709, but attracted little attention. It was the Montgolfier brothers' experiments in 1782 and 1783 that brought this technology to the world's attention.

The first successful manned flight was in a balloon on 21 November 1783. Pilatre de Rozier and the Marquis d'Arlandes travelled more than eight kilometres at 3,000 feet in a hot-air balloon constructed by Joseph Michel Montgolfier and his brother Jacques Étienne. Ten days later, the French physicist Jacques Charles and M. Robert took off from les Tuileries, Paris, in a bathtub shaped gondola under a hydrogen-filled balloon.

There were various inventors who attempted flight but it took another 120 years before a heavier-than-air flying machine got off the ground, but only just.

1903 17 December, U.S., Orville and Wilbur Wright made the first flight in a heavier-than-air machine. They flew for a distance of 36.5 metres, at an altitude of three metres.

1906 22 October, France, the Brazilian Alberto Santos-Dumont flew for a distance 60 metres at an altitude of three metres.

1908 16 October, England, the American Samuel Franklin Cody flew 423 metres at an altitude of 5.5 metres.

1909 23 February, Canada, Douglas McCurdy flew Bell's *Silver Dart* 800 metres at an altitude of nine metres.[19]

1911 5 July, Graham Gilmour flew a Bristol bi-plane over London.
9 September, first ever aerial post delivery from Hendon to Windsor Castle.[20]

1915 During the First World War, the first Zeppelin attack on London took place in June.

1919 14 June, 5:00 p.m., Captain John Alcock and Arthur W. Brown took off from Newfoundland. They landed in Ireland 15 June, 9:12 a.m. It is the first non-stop transatlantic flight.

1924 First flight from England to India. It took 220 hours.

1927 May, Lindbergh flew solo from New York to Paris in 37 hours.

1937 Amelia Earhart is lost on her cross-Pacific flight.

1944 First non-stop flight from London to Canada.

1947 First supersonic flight.

> **1934 Air Navigation**. A more recent invention is the aeroplane, already of economic importance in the transportation of passengers and supplies to new and remote mining areas etc. The mileage flown by aircraft increased from 185,000 in 1922 to 4,569,131 in 1932 when 76,800 passengers, 3,129,974 pounds of freight or express, and 413,687 pounds of mail were carried.[21]

Those were the years when flying was new and exciting, when the transatlantic Pan Am Clipper (a flying boat)

Flying came of age in the First World War. Courtesy of the Collection of Al Albania.

made regular landings in Shediac Bay because it gets very little fog, unlike most of the coast, and glamorous and exotic passengers disembarked.

Then the war started, and we entertained countless airmen-in-training. The talk was of Hurricanes and later Spitfires, Wellingtons, and Lancasters. The ferry pilots flew bombers across the Atlantic via Greenland and Iceland, and by the time the war ended, flying was a familiar form of travel.

For a complete story of flight in Canada, see Peter Pigott, *On Canadian Wings: A Century of Flight* (Toronto: Dundurn Press, 2007). For the wartime experience, Ian Darling, *Amazing Airmen: Canadian Flyers in the Second World War* (Toronto: Dundurn Press, 2009). For more on railways and how they developed, see John Westwood, *Historical Atlas of World Railroads* (Toronto: Firefly, 2008).

Chapter 8

Trades
and Their Tools

Every human being born into the world will find that
happiness mainly depends upon the work that he does
and the manner in which it is done…. the choice of a
trade is a most important event in every boy's life.[1]

Learning a Trade

In 1999, Leonard G. Lee of Lee Valley Tools reprinted the
1865 edition of *The Boy's Book of Trades and the Tools Used
in Them.* Lee tells us that this book "draws together a great
deal of information on trades that have long since vanished." Actually, they have not vanished so much as changed
methods and machinery. Consider a few surnames: Smith,
Forger, Miller/Meunier, Potter/Potier, Baker/Boulanger. In
fact, you can play this game in most languages.

The book's original purpose was to tell boys about the
many trades they could enter as an apprentice. In North

America, we do not have the established tradition of apprenticeship that exists in Britain and Europe, but these definitions outline the boy's learning curve:

> **apprentice** — a person who is learning a trade by being employed in it for an agreed period of time at a low wage. When the apprentice has worked his allotted time and his master thinks he is qualified, he becomes a journeyman. The trade guild or association may also set conditions.
>
> **journeyman** — a fully trained mechanic or artisan who works for another. He may have to work for some years before he has acquired enough capital to set up in business for himself. Again the guild or association may set standards of workmanship for becoming a master of the trade.
>
> **master** — a person skilled in a particular trade and qualified to teach others, e.g. master carpenter, master mariner.[2]

The trades listed in *The Boy's Book* start with building construction, and include many still practised today, although now we have power tools, assembly lines, and new materials. Even by 1865, quite a number of trades were starting to change from totally hands-on work to machine-assisted labour, however they don't mention the treadle or crank-operated sewing machine as tailor's tools. They existed at the time, but were not part of the traditional way things were done.

In 1865, brickmakers still moulded each brick individually, though there were mechanical aids for preparing the clay. Masons cut and shaped each piece of stone using mallets, chisels, wedges, and a type of hammer called a "beetle." Setting the shaped stones in place was "properly part of his work." We no longer build entirely in stone, and today's mason probably provides only ornamental surfaces, but restoring our heritage buildings — be they a lock master's cottage or the Houses of Parliament — still demands such skills.

A bricklayer's work has changed over the centuries from building the entire wall to providing a surface facing of bricks. Wallboard has displaced the plasterer, and finding one who can restore the elaborate cornices and ceiling medallions in a Victorian house is difficult.

The carpenter and joiner, housepainter and glazier are still at work. Strictly speaking, carpentry may be defined as the framing and structural work on a building, while the joiner is concerned with the woodwork fitting and finishings such as doors, windows, panelling, stairs, skirtings, and architraves, both in their preparation in the workshop and installing them on the building site.[3]

Lead Workers

Plumber comes from the Latin word for lead, *plumbum*. Plumbers in 1850 did very different work from that of today's well-paid tradesmen. To start with, they needed to be able "to go up a ladder or look over a ledge at a height from the ground without being afraid."[4] That is because the first plumbers made the leaden roofs of churches and public buildings. The plumber and glazier were often one and the same, since they made the windows where lead strips held the little diamond-shaped panes of glass. A glazier still replaces broken panes of glass, but usually in wooden frames.

Housepainters also worked with lead: white lead formed the base of most paints. There is a gentle warning: "Unfortunately, while it is in the half-fluid state, when it is used by Painters, it is very poisonous and unwholesome, and many workmen suffer severely in their health from its use."[5]

Change was on the way in 1865:

> The Plumbers do not make quite so many leaden casements as they made in the olden time, but they are well employed in constructing roofs; carrying water into houses by means of leaden pipes; making cisterns to contain a good supply of it, and providing other pipes and gutters for conveying all the dirty water and drainage into the sewers that are under the roadway, where it runs quite away from the streets.[6]

The gasfitter also worked with lead pipes, as well as those made from iron and brass. His trade was important when there were "few large houses … not lighted by gas."[7] The technologies have changed, but since many households are still heated by gas, and some use it for cooking, we still have gasfitters.

Smith Is a Common Name

A smith works with metal. Goldsmiths and silversmiths work with the most precious, blacksmiths and whitesmiths (or tinsmiths) with the more common elements, iron and tin. Britain has mineral resources, which it has exploited since the Bronze Age. Working any metal has its own techniques, or "mysteries," and the old trades persist today.

- The ironfounder supplied the blacksmith of 1865 with malleable iron, so he could make the various articles of wrought iron once used in buildings: "pileshoes, straps, screw bolts, dog-irons, chimney-bars, gratings, and wrought iron railings and balustrades for staircases."[8] However by 1865, cast iron had replaced wrought iron for many purposes.

- Today we think of a blacksmith doing the work of a farrier, who specializes in shoeing horses, but originally he only supplied the shoe.

- The brassfounder made the alloy of copper and zinc called brass; in earlier years, he probably also made the copper and tin alloy called bronze. The bronzesmith crafted these easily cast or worked metals, sometimes making domestic utensils and small items, like buttons, horse brasses, and the small fittings "such as catches, locks, bolts, hooks, screws" used in furnishing a house. These men might, at times, be called upon to found large bells for a church.

- The coppersmith worked with copper, perhaps making wire, or pots and pans for the kitchen, or covering the bottoms of wooden ships with thin sheets of the metal to protect them from marine worms. Copper has a multitude of uses, and today's craftspeople and jewellers sometimes use it when gold or silver is too costly.

• A tinman, what *The Boy's Book* calls a tin-smith or whitesmith, works with tin, the most easily melted of all the common metals. Tin plate is sheet iron coated on both sides with a layer of tin. The copper kitchenware made by coppersmiths must all be tinned on the inside to be safe for cooking, and tin is the primary ingredient in pewter and such white-metal alloys as Britannia metal, which are used for domestic articles such as platters, tankards, and candlesticks.

Special Trades

The trade of cutler, or cutting-instrument maker, is an ancient one. Swords and knife blades are best made from steel, which was once made by heating iron weapons over red-hot charcoal so the carbon was absorbed, definitely a craft "mystery" until 1740 when the "crucible" method of making steel was developed in Sheffield. That city was noted for metal work of all sorts and it was there that an early technique for plating copper with a thin layer of silver was developed.

Another specialist was the cooper; he made casks and barrels. He had to be a skilled wood worker, making the staves and fitting them together into a barrel shape, then binding them with wooden or iron hoops. Many such containers had to be capable of holding liquids, such as wine or beer, strong enough to withstand the jolting of transportation, as well as the pressure created by fermentation. It was definitely a craft, with many "tricks of the trade" to learn.

A house has to be furnished. Cabinetmakers and upholsterers may now use power tools, but their work is similar to that done in historical times. However, I suspect any gilder who still puts real gold leaf on elaborate picture frames now works in a conservation laboratory.

A chandler originally dealt in candles and wax, but later in all sorts of groceries and supplies. Today's chandlery usually supplies ships or yachtsmen.

The chapman, or pedlar, travelled about the country selling small domestic articles to country housewives, along with fabrics, tapes, ribbons, and whatever else the market demanded. In his travels, he might encounter teams of four to eight drovers driving large herds of cattle, often over long distances to urban markets. Drovers were essentially cattle dealers. Other common trade-names fed, and still feed us: hunter and fisher, then farmer, miller, and baker.

- The flesher, or butcher, killed and cut up animals (and might not have left their trade-names to as many progeny), but once the hide was off the animal the tanner commenced his work.

- The age-old process of turning hides into leather, we are told in *The Boy's Book*, "has received less alteration from recent improvements in chemical science than many other manufacturing processes."[9]

- A currier is the person who dresses and colours tanned leather, "by which the requisite smoothness, lustre, colour and suppleness are imparted."[10]

- Tawing is the process that converts the skins of lambs or kids into soft leather for gloves by the application of alum.

- The glover worked with many different leathers. The "mystery" of his craft was the knowledge of how to cut and assemble the variously shaped pieces, the thumb piece, fourchettes, and gussets, to fit the hand.

- Saddlers and the harness makers used the tanner's and brassmith's products for elegant equipage. Much of the work consisted of sewing, and while various leathers required different techniques, a hole had to be punched for each stitch. An apprentice had much to learn.

- The tanner's other customer was the shoemaker, or to use the medieval term, cordwainer. A cobbler is someone who repaired shoes: the verb "to cobble" means to mend, patch up, or put together without much skill, so presumably a cobbler does not have the skills of a master shoemaker. "Scarcely any handicraft employment engages the attention of so many persons in this country as boot and shoe making."[11]

The Boy's Book goes on to describe the production in which different parts were made by separate groups of workers, sometimes in different countries, and the several elements were put together in a sort of assembly line process by workers skilled in one or another procedure.

Factories now do much of the work once done by the traditional tanner, shoemaker, and saddler, as well as the tailor and glover. However, in all trades there are still skilled specialists who do custom work; the same is true of millers and bakers. *The Boy's Book* lists some other factory-based trades now totally mechanised, such as cotton manufacturer, calico printer, calenderer, hotpresser, paper stainer (wallpaper maker), file cutter, sugar refiner, floor cloth manufacturer, gun manufacturer, and needle maker.

Making Cloth

The cloth trade, especially the preparation of wool, has been an important part of Britain's economy for centuries. The wool clip must be cleaned and the fleece carded so that the fibres are more or less parallel for spinning. The thread is then woven on a loom by a weaver, and the cloth fulled (cleansed and thickened) by a fuller. Carders and spinners were mostly women, which may explain why they are less familiar surnames. Limited production of cotton cloth in England began around 1600, but it wasn't until a century later that it began to challenge the primacy of wool. As its importance grew, cotton spinning and weaving of cotton became some of the earliest crafts to be mechanised.

The dyer may colour the uncarded fleece, the spun thread, or the woven cloth, and this age-old art was commonly practised in large dye works. Changing the colour of clothing — often to black for mourning — was done in small custom shops. Thanks to Tintex and other easy-to-use package dyes, such changes could be done at home by the 1920s. The expert dyer was still around in the 1960s, but the advent of nylon, polyesters, and mixed-fibre fabrics ended most custom and home dying. Dyes work somewhat differently with silk, wool, cotton, and linen, but very differently with some synthetics. Centuries-old knowledge no longer applies, and old techniques don't work on certain fibre mixes.

French weavers produced a lot of silk, but there was a small, government-protected trade in England. Some patterned fabric was woven at Spitalfields, but most workers made the silk ribbons to trim the caps and hats every fashionable woman wore. All across Europe, lace was a part of any fashionable woman's wardrobe, and also of most men's until the nineteenth century. Making lace was one of a few home-based trades a woman could pursue. The history of lace and lace making has filled more than one book.

Deadly Trades

As you travel back into your ancestor's times, you will become aware of how much shorter their lives were than our own. What you may not realize at first, is that it was not only infections that were deadly, but also their work itself.

- Today we know about, and protect workers from, the dangers of lead and mercury poisoning, and the damage various kinds of dusts, especially silicone, can do to the lungs, the perils of breathing chemical fumes, and the danger of accidents with unshielded machinery. Almost all the workers mentioned above were exposed to one or more of these dangers, and many probably died because of them.

- One of the first new skills required by the Industrial Revolution and its steam engines would have been that of the boilermaker. It was a dangerous, often deadly, trade — as were any of the jobs using steam under pressure in closed containers. Some of the first brotherhoods (early trade unions) were formed among railway workers as a means of securing life insurance for engine drivers, firemen, and brakemen.

- Forestry was another field of work where accidents were common. The sawyer and feller had to be skilled at "hurling down the pine," so that the tree did not fall on them or their fellows, but there were many accidents. In North America, the timber was cut in the winter, then when the ice went out of the rivers, the log drives began to the booms or sawmills. Log-drivers might "learn to step lightly," but they risked their lives daily.[12]

Lumbering, shipbuilding, and sailing were all dangerous occupations. Some of my ancestors worked in these trades; the reports of accidental deaths add a sorrowful note to family histories. The *Saint John Daily Telegraph* of 25 June 1872, reported:

... a very sad and fatal accident occurred
in the shipyard of James H. Moran Esq.,
Quaco by which Mr. Henry Smith, the
much respected foreman of the yard lost
his life. Mr. Smith who was a gentleman of
about 65 years of age and had long worked
in the yard, was engaged on the keel of the
new vessel which Mr. Moran had just commenced. Not far from him was an upright
the end of which had got loosened and was
only slightly held. Owing to something
coming in contact with it, that heavy piece
of timber fell in the direction in which Mr.
Smith was working. An alarm was given ere
it reached the ground, but too late to save
Mr. Smith, though two other men escaped
the blow. It fell upon his head and left side,
crushing his head, his ribs and his heart.[13]

We are told that "Medical assistance was called and Dr.
Ruddick was soon found ... but neither medical aid nor
kindly sympathy was of any avail."

The account records that "one of his sons, Captain
Henry Smith is now at Rangoon." That son lost his life
four years later. In 1876, early in November, severe storms
were reported in India; his ship, the *Prince Waldemar*, was
stranded on the "Boldering Sands in the Hoogly River" on
a voyage from Liverpool to Calcutta. Captain Smith, his
wife Eleanor, and their two small children lost their lives
along with most of the crew.[14]

Following the trail of a shipping fleet in the Board of
Trade's Register of Shipping turns up many accounts of lost

ships.[15] Now and then there is a happy ending, as in the tale of the *Masonic* (no. 64465), a 177.52 ton brigantine built at St. Martins by John Carson and launched 10 August 1870.

> Vessel left Sydney Cape Breton 20 Dec. 1870 with a cargo of coal for this port [Saint John, N.B.] & has not been heard of. Supposed to have been lost. Registry closed the 20th February 1871.
>
> Vessel turned up all right, was driven off the coast and ran down to Guadaloupe from thence proceeded to St. Thomas, Puerto Rico, & New York. Restored to her former Registry[16]

After a winter in the sun of the West Indies, instead of the storms of the north Atlantic, we learn that George Bell of Dublin was empowered to sell her. Before he could, the *Masonic* was abandoned at sea on 14 December 1872 in a sinking condition. She was on a voyage from Dorchester, New Brunswick, to Boston, Massachusetts, with a cargo of brownstone. The crew was saved by a Dutch vessel and taken to Boston, and the registry was closed 5 February 1873.[17] The crew undoubtedly found other New Brunswick ships in Boston to bring them home — so they could risk their lives once again.

Chapter 9

Work Away From Home

For men must work, and women must weep,
And there's little to earn, and many to keep.[1]

That was true in 1858 — C.E or B.C.E (A.D. or B.C.)
— and it's still true. Men and women have to leave home
to earn a living. Sometimes it is the nature of the job: soldiers, sailors, fishermen, oil-rig workers, airline pilots, or
truckers. Then there are servants and caregivers who leave
poor countries to work in rich ones. Now and then, it is
the sheer love of adventure that moves people: "Something
hidden. Go and find it."[2]

Nevertheless, in exploring your past, you should be
aware of the many occupations that required workers to
be away from home when the census was taken. You can
read more about this in my *Here Be Dragons, too!* Here are
some new ideas.

Transient and Temporary

Young, unskilled men can go wherever a strong arm and back are needed. If canals are being dug, roads and railways built, or wood is being cut, jobs are there for a season or two. Transient, temporary farm labour has always been needed to harvest crops, and in North America, lumber camps provided winter work and cash for farmers and their sons. In the late nineteenth and early twentieth century, "harvest trains" took boys from the East, out West to help with the wheat harvest. We still employ migrant workers to pick fruit in Ontario.

- In the censuses from 1851–52 and 1861, your farmer ancestor's name may appear with the comment "in shanty." Those tallies were taken in January when he was working in the woods cutting timber. The men lived in log shanties provided by the company. Lumber-camp food was hearty, but usually tasty, since a good cook attracted the best workers.[3]

- Cattle boats needed extra hands to care for the beef-on-the-hoof (cattle that were brought from the West by train, then fattened on farms in the East) being shipped to England. A lot of young men saw the world, not as sailors, but by using the skills they had learned on their home farm. It was not first-class travel but it got you across the Atlantic.

Skills Are Portable

If the someone who left was in their twenties, try to discover if he or she had a trade. Skilled workers, as well as good cooks, go wherever the work is, or adventure calls.

- Blacksmiths were always in demand. They might have wintered in the lumber camps, then followed the canals or railways as they were being constructed in summer. Any project that used teams of horses always needed a blacksmith.

- The nineteenth century saw a lot of jobs disappear as industries changed, and old technologies were replaced by new. A lot of work was mechanized, but machines have to be maintained and repaired. Think how a skill might adapt to new enterprises and changed conditions.

- Stone masons were needed to build all the canals, not just houses. Millwrights and others with mechanical skills would be in demand wherever machinery was being used — and abused.

- Shipwrights were usually skilled woodworkers, and when that industry died around the Great Lakes and in the Maritimes, many found work building wooden cars for the new railways. That would mean moving from a shipyard on the coast into the towns where the railway shops were located.

- Miners also have portable skills. In 1849, news of "Gold in California!" brought the first large groups of Chinese migrant workers to North America. In the Chinese language, the characters for California can also be read as "Gold Mountain," which soon became the term for much of west coast North America.

- A decade later, gold was discovered in British Columbia and many of the Chinese miners went north, and the first Chinatowns sprang up. Until 1884, immigrants from China were permitted to enter and leave Canada without restrictions.

- In the early twentieth century, as the mineral wealth of the Laurentian shield was discovered, young men brought mining skills from European countries to Northern Ontario.

- Almost all such arrivals, Chinese or European, were young, single men. Those who were married left their wives and families back home, dreaming of returning with a fortune, or hoping to earn enough to pay their family's passage at a later date.

What about Women?

As the nineteenth century ended, employment opportunities for women were limited. For those with education there were the old standbys, nursing and teaching, and newer ones in business, such as typists or telephone operators. Those with fewer advantages found work as domestic servants. Sewing was also a female skill.

- Nursing and teaching often took young women away from their homes. Hospitals had nurses' residences, and teachers might live with family, friends, or the families of the pupils, sometimes living in several households over a school year. Room and board could be part of her salary, and the way the host family paid their school taxes.

- Dressmakers had portable skills, and while many were able to work at home, since a large town might provide an adequate customer base, some went from home to home, spending a few weeks making up the new wardrobe for the women of the household.

- Some women left home hoping to find employment as servants in the city or even in a new country, but they could also earn their living by working in shops, garment factories, or for milliners. Until the 1850s, when the sewing machine was perfected, every garment was stitched entirely by hand. Even with machine assistance, there was a lot of sewing to be done on flounced crinolines.

- When the first practical and efficient

mechanical typewriter was patented in 1868, it only printed capital letters. The shift key came along 10 years later, and in 1883 another technological breakthrough allowed the typist to see the page as it was being printed. A woman who learned to be a "typewriter" could earn her own living, and business schools began to teach these skills.

- By the 1920s, every young girl was advised to learn to touch type; it assured her of a job in one of the countless office typing pools. Learning shorthand allowed the office worker to take dictation, so she could become the secretary to some executive. If she were smart, she might even join the lower levels of office management.

- Male secretaries were better paid, and had greater chance of promotion. Railway officials, politicians, and anyone who travelled regularly would usually have a male secretary who could travel with them, since a woman could not.

- It was the Second World War that brought an end to the rule that many employers had, stating that women should give up their jobs when they married. Before that, a woman could have a job, or a husband, but in most instances the two did not go together. Widows, however, could work.

Professional and Business Migrants

- Teachers could change schools many times, but usually remained within a regional education system (in Canada, provincial).

- Clergymen were also very mobile, but most denominations have annual directories that list each man and his charge. Normally clergymen lived in houses owned by the local church.

- Doctors, who might start a practice in a rural community far from their homes, sometimes returned later in their careers to big-city hospitals where they had friends and contacts. If they also taught, mobility went with the job.

- Bank managers and accountants moved regularly. Typically, the banks owned houses in town for their branch managers, while the accountant might live in an apartment over the bank, as a matter of security. The bank clerks were usually young men, almost always single, working their way up in the profession as they moved from branch to branch gaining experience, but never staying anywhere long enough to fiddle the books. When banks began to use female staff, for the most part they hired young ladies or widows living in the town.

Transportation Workers

After 1840, railways provided work for thousands of men and some women. They also allowed other workers to live farther from their work places, and commute daily or weekly. This applies particularly to the professional and business migrants, discussed above.

- On both sides of the Atlantic, people found new jobs running the trains, as well as the stations, yards, and telegraph lines, and maintaining tracks along every route. Young railway workers tended to move from small to large towns, in the hope of better jobs and pay.

- Employees who preferred to settle down in one place could accumulate seniority, enabling them to do so. Others could remain transients all their working life, but a few might make it to head office.

- Skilled craftsmen could find employment in the industries that supplied the engines, cars, rails, and other equipment. Wherever railways spread their networks, expect to find young men leaving farms to become apprentices in the big railway shops, which, in Canada, were in Moncton, Montreal, Stratford, and Winnipeg.

- North American railways, and most of their trade unions, were continental in scope. Their operating divisions ignored provincial and state borders, and paid little heed to the 49th parallel — except to take on an immigration or customs crew. Employees of Canadian lines worked in the States; employees of American lines worked in Canada. That means the records you want may be in the U.S., not Canada.

- Remember that railway companies also owned hotels and shipping lines, which employed thousands of workers who might be transferred often.

- Railways and families go together. A youth might start as apprentice to his father or uncle, learn the trade, and become a master mechanic, master car builder, road master, or he might attain a major position in the trade brotherhood. He would then be expected to find jobs for the next generation of the family, even quite distant cousins. If one member of a family worked for the railroad, expect to find others.

Two Homes to be Away From

The railways called them "running trades"; the engineers, conductors, brakemen, firemen, and sleeping-car porters, might have two homes, one at each end of their run. The sailors and steamship staff led a similar life, but with longer runs. Postal clerks, as well as immigration and customs crews, also worked on trains. Like the running trades, they would have a regular run with a home at one end and a second bed at the away end. These men were employed by federal government departments, and between 1868 and 1926 they might be listed in the Dominion of Canada Sessional Papers.[4]

The Call of the Wilds

Hopes of fortune and the lure of the wilderness have been drawing people across the Atlantic since the time of Saint Brendan. For a couple of centuries, the Hudson's Bay Company operating out of London, England, and the North West Company based in Montreal offered work to satisfy both longings. The Hudson's Bay Company took over its rival in 1821. For a detailed discussion of these Bay Men, North Westers, and their Aboriginal companions (or "country wives") see chapters 5 and 6 of *Here Be Dragons, too!* The following notes tell you about the records.

- In 1670, Charles II granted his cousin Prince Rupert and his Company of Adventurers a monopoly over trade and mineral rights in all the lands draining into Hudson Bay. Thus was born the Hudson's Bay Company, which established "factories" from Labrador to the Rockies, and well below the 49th parallel.

- The Company hired literate young men who wrote a fine hand as clerks, favouring men from the northern islands of the United Kingdom who were used to long winter nights and lack of sunlight. They learned the trade in the wilderness of Rupert's Land. From the seventeenth through to the twentieth century, most

Bay Men who survived to retirement age usually went home to the U.K.

• Even after Confederation, when Rupert's Land was sold to the new Dominion, the Hudson's Bay Company remained a huge enterprise. It also documented all of their employees' activities. The company's superb and extensive archives are now held by the Government of Manitoba as a division of the provincial archives in Winnipeg, which posts information and finding aids on the Internet.

• In 1898, gold was discovered in Bonanza Creek, which runs into the Klondike River, and tens of thousands of hopeful prospectors poured into the Northwest. Provisioners, entertainers, clergy, police, and judiciary followed, as did Dominion land surveyors. When the gold ran out, the Yukon Territorial Government remained. The Yukon Archives still preserves a wealth of records from this era. Moreover, this gold rush occurred during the era of photography, so there are splendid visual records.

• On 14 April 1872, the first Dominion Lands Act laid out the policy of free quarter-section homestead grants. This made a farm in the Canadian West an achievable dream. The results of this and subsequent acts are Homestead Records (c.1885–1930) with nominal indexes listing land locations. Files may provide information on the applicant's age, marital status, number of children, place of birth, employment (both on the homestead and during absences) value of improvements, dates of entry, and patent.

Evacuees, Displaced People, and War Brides

Wars displace people and families. Regardless of which war or revolution it was, you can expect to find some of your ancestors moving about in times of conflict. Perhaps a few hundred miles to another job in a new city, perhaps halfway around the world.

Henry Adelbert "Harry" Chapman — one of the young boys in the group photo on page 163 — joined the Canadian Expeditionary Forces during the First World War and found a bride in England. He and Helen Williams were married in England in June 1917. After the war, they returned to Canada with their baby daughter, Althea, to farm in Alberta. Image Courtesy of Don Chapman.

- The end of the Second World War and the ensuing Cold War brought about a huge migration of displaced people from all across Europe. Some were political refugees, but many had been forced to leave their homes when their towns or villages had been destroyed. They could not return because home no longer existed.

- Canada welcomed a lot of these DPs. At the time, "DP" did not have a derogatory connotation any more than "boat people" had when we welcomed refugees from Viet Nam. The terms were simply a quick explanation of a tragic situation most Canadians understood and sympathized with. They became the latest New Canadians — just as the Loyalists had in 1783.

- Young soldiers fall in love. During both World Wars, more than a few Canadian soldiers fell in love, married, and eventually brought their spouses back to Canada. A recent book, *War Brides* by Melynda Jarratt, tells some of these stories from the Second World War.[5]

- Many immigrants arrived in Canada at Pier 21 in Halifax, Nova Scotia. The Pier 21 Museum opened in 1999 and now offers assistance to researchers by email, post, telephone, or in person. Its holdings include an oral history and story collection, an image collection, and a number of databases.[6]

- During the Second World War, there was another displaced group: the British children who were evacuated to North America at a formative time of their life and education. Their story is told by Jessica Mann in her extensively researched book *Out Of Harm's Way: The Wartime Evacuation of Children from Britain.*[7]

Home Children and Residential Schools

Trying to do what is best for somebody else often evokes the Law of Unintended Consequences. Two such endeavours in the late nineteenth century, which began with the best of intentions, had unfortunate consequences for a tragic number of children. We are only now coming to understand and regret these ventures.

The Home Children, sent overseas from Britain "to a new life," and Aboriginal children removed from their families and communities to be educated and integrated into "civilized society" have been studied and documented, and are two more groups of displaced people.

- In Britain the Industrial Revolution brought slums, unhealthy living conditions, and a population of urban poor where mortality was high. There were a lot of orphans and uncared for children. People with the best of intentions founded orphanages and homes and tried hard to "rescue and educate" these unfortunates.

- Quite a number of these children were sent overseas to the British Dominions (Australia, Canada), where local branches of various charities handed them over to local families, many of whom saw these ragamuffins as cheap labour.

- In most colonies, the first schools for Aboriginal people were founded by missionaries, primarily from the Roman Catholic, Anglican, and Methodist churches, sometimes with Imperial government support. They were rarely part of the pre-Confederation education systems.[8]

- Since 1867, the federal government, through the Department of Indian Affairs, has had theoretical jurisdiction and responsibility for education on reserves. Very little was actually done until almost the end of the First World War. The earliest school records in RG10 (Library and Archives Record Group for the Department of Indian Affairs) date from around 1916.

- Boarding schools, many run by churches, were where a lot of well-to-do Canadians sent their children to be educated. When such people were making decisions about what was the best way to educate children on remote and scattered Native reserves they came up with the same idea:

    Residential schools — schools established to teach the Indian

children who were removed from
the custody of their parents to res-
ide in that institution.[9]

Some of the uprooted children, both Home Children
and Aboriginal, were well cared for and educated, but
many had very unhappy experiences, which are only now
coming to light.

But How Do I Prove It?

*The young man who moves prior to his marriage is
perhaps the most difficult of all migrants to trace and
identify with certainty.*[10]

If your family tree includes refugees from the devastation
of a war, you might dispute this, but the problem posed
is similar:

- Just because you have found two people
  with the same name, the first in Place A in
  one year — who then vanishes — and the
  second in Place B a year later, *does not prove*
  that they are one and the same person.

- Known facts about the person in the place
  of destination (age, birthday, parent's
  names) must agree with data on the person
  at the place of origin before you can even
  begin to speculate that they could be one
  person who moved from Place A to Place B.

Who Stayed Behind?

In rural communities, older sons frequently grew to manhood while their father was still active and in charge of the farm. Even a prosperous farm cannot support five or six families, so it was the oldest sons who tended to leave home to make their fortunes elsewhere, in a nearby city or a distant homestead, mine, or shop.

Young adults who moved away from the family home, for whatever reason, usually left siblings, parents, or relatives behind. If you have information about the family he or she left in Place A, you might start by looking into what went on in Place A in later years.

- It was often the younger children who cared for ageing parents and ended up inheriting the family homestead. This can show up in either probate or land transfer documents, in which the older siblings, now living in another province, state or even country, have to agree to some arrangement and send notarized documents, many years after they left home.

- Sometimes, when they have done well, the elder brothers and/or their families come home for a visit, perhaps to attend a family wedding or funeral. It is worth checking the Social Notes in local newspapers for information on who came from where to attend such family events.

- Weekly local papers are the family historian's best friend. Before female equality was politically correct they had Women's Pages and Social Pages. There were stringers in surrounding villages who sent in the Notes of Our Town. You can frequently learn whose daughter or sister was visiting from which big city or small town.

Our social conventions on death notices have changed, as well. Most death notices from the last quarter of the twentieth century are sadly uninformative. Things have improved a bit in this century but one longs for the good old days.

- Before the Second World War, when someone of any prominence died, the local paper would carry a report of the funeral, who attended to pay their last respects, and who sent floral tributes. This news would appear within a day or two (or in the next weekly issue).

- Don't stop looking. A later issue of the same newspapers would almost certainly carry an obituary detailing the deceased person's career, parents, family, and descendants, but this tribute might take a week or so to write. As well, Social Notes would tell of relatives coming from distant parts, and probably remaining in the area for a few weeks visiting with several families in the region.

Connections Matter

Whether you are concerned primarily with Place A or Place B, if documentary evidence is sparse, the proof may be in *connections*: grandmother's cousin, the aunt of a family friend, the sister-in-law of a next-door neighbour. Those sorts of links between families, friends, and neighbours are often the clues you need. Who lived nearby? Who attended a wedding? Do any of the people in Place B come from Place A originally? Chain migration was also very common.

- Search beyond census reports and obituaries. Check all vital statistics, *both* civil registrations and church records, and be sure to note any other places or people associated with the event in question. For example, who signed the marriage bond? The names of witnesses or sponsors can be helpful bits of the puzzle.

- Be sure to continue your search through the parish registers for other events involving the same people. There might be notes on those who signed: brother, uncle of the bride, grandfather of the baby.

- If two couples were married at the same time, even if the surnames are different, they might have been cousins. Keep an eye out for other couples baptising children at the same time — they may be related.

- Never limit your research to immediate family surnames. Women marry, change their names, and if the first husband dies, often marry again and add yet another name.

- Look for land records. Wives had dower rights, and often had to sign them over, look for *et ux* (and wife) in any index to deeds. That clause will give you the wife's name — often the proof you need.

Gather as much evidence from as many sources as you can. With luck, the pieces of the puzzle will fit and you will have your proof. Two books, Brenda Merriman's *About Genealogical Standards of Evidence* (Toronto: OGS/ Dundurn, 2010) and Elizabeth Shown Mills's *Evidence! Citation and Analysis for the Family Historian* (Baltimore: Genealogical Publishing, 1997) are both excellent guides to evaluating what you find.

Chapter 10

Family and Connections

Follow the Female Line

The profession of genealogy, with those quaintly named Heralds and Kings of Arms, grew out of the need for a feudal society to keep track of who held land, and so who was obliged to fight for the king. Daughters did not fight, so it was the man they married who mattered and the sons they bore who inherited the estates.

Does the female line matter? To the genealogical purist, perhaps not; but it is usually the women in a family who cherish heirlooms, recount family legends, and preserve traditions, not to mention letters, documents, and artifacts. Knowledge of family networks can aid in finding treasures from the past.

> **An Example**: Fanny (Burney) d'Arblay, the novelist you met in Chapter 6, left her papers

to her niece, Charlotte (Francis) Barrett, who passed them on to her daughter Julia (Barrett) Thomas Maitland, and so to Julia (Maitland) Wauchope and the Wauchope children. It took Dr. Joyce Hemlow, from Nova Scotia, to follow that female line and unearth the treasured papers from under Miss Ann Julia Wauchope's bed.

Connectional History

Useful knowledge as well as family treasures pass down the female line. As a child I listened to my mother and her friends gossip as they played bridge or sewed for the Red Cross.

Almost every person they mentioned was identified by a place, then by two or three family connections. "She was a T—— from Dorchester, a sister married one of the B——s from Amherst, or was he the McL—— son? His mother was a R—— from Halifax." The links they spoke of might be blood or marriage; a few were simply "they lived next door and we grew up together." I visualized a great spider web that connected everyone in the Maritimes, with anchor lines stretching off to Montreal and Toronto, down to Boston, and west to the Pacific coast.

Looking back I can recognize the purpose of that conversational pattern. For my mother's generation, born at the turn of the twentieth century, and often far away from family, it reinforced their knowledge of the wider community. With men, it's easy. Father, son, uncle, brother — all have the same surname so the connections are obvious. It is the women, who change their name on marriage, who must be kept track of.

- It is with other women's help that you establish a social life in a new community when a banker or railroader husband is moved there or who knows where, to find a reliable housekeeper for a widowed father back home. That is why it is women who usually maintained the links.

- The place name associated with a family served not only to distinguish the Yarmouth Killams from the family of the Westmorland County M.P., it also reminded the younger generation where their roots lay.

- Compact regions, long-settled by inter-related families exist everywhere in the world. Quebec's Eastern Townships and Ontario's Ottawa Valley are such places.

Families and connections: Cavour Chapman and Fred Tenant built summer cottages beside each other on Shediac Bay. Three generations of their descendants clambered over these cliffs as childhood friends.

Like Maritimers, Township and Valley people usually know who each other's grandmothers were.

Kin Groups

To an anthropologist, a "kin group" is a band of primates or tribe of humans sharing the same genes, who cooperate to ensure those genes are passed on to as many in future generations as possible. The natural size of such a kin group is between 50 and 200 individuals.[1] That could be the population of a small village or early settlement. British genealogist, Stella Colwell, discussing her kin group in the Lake District explains how it still works today:

> The effective kinship network of living relatives … offered financial support, help in obtaining work and accommodation, and provided contacts for relatives working away from home, material support for the elderly and newly married, a child minding service, assistance and wholesale attendance at family events and a host of other supportive acts. They also split into factions carrying grievances along the family network.[2]

Kin groups are helpful and function much the same way everywhere. However, their size can vary with time and place.

- In Britain and Europe, until the late nineteenth century, the more affluent tended to have larger families than the poor. They could afford to marry younger; it could also be related to better nutrition. Whatever the number of children, a mother could expect to lose at least one in three before they were a year old, and probably another by age 10.

- Across the Atlantic, demographic researchers are finding that in the early pioneer communities "infant mortality was low. At least 75 percent of the children survived to adulthood. This was very different from Europe."[3] Fertility was higher than in Europe, too. There was a lot more protein available to settlers who could hunt and fish in the forests and streams, free from gamekeepers and laws against poaching.

Family Size

Until well into the twentieth century, family historians can expect to find records showing that married women tended to have a baby every two to three years. If a married woman lived to age 50, she could expect to bear 10 to 15 children.

- A man looking at families of this size is likely to think "Ah, six sons to carry on the name." Or, more practically, "more hands to help with haying, chores, and clearing the land."

- A woman looking at the same line will think "Six boys to feed and keep in clothes" — lucky she had daughters to help.

- Considering the potatoes to peel, the wool to spin and weave, the colic and croup, most women will also wonder about the wife's support network. Did she have family nearby, her mother, sisters, or in-laws to help in an emergency?

Fifty Cousins

Often the first settlers had little support, but the next generation was far better off. Using a conservative estimate of eight surviving children per family, assume that six of those children married, each into another eight-child family. That's a lot of in-laws. A sister-in-law's family, or even *her* in-laws, might be called upon to help. Move to the third generation: even if those six couples averaged only five children each, each child would have 25 cousins on their father's side, 25 more on their mother's, which makes 50 cousins all told.

You can expect most of the cousins to marry; their families make a large kin group. Divorce was rare, but death in childbirth, at sea, or in the woods, meant there were almost as many second and even third marriages as today. A newcomer marrying into such a family would have to learn who were the cousins to be cultivated and which n'er-do-wells to avoid. A few who returned to New or Old England, or who went West, for example, might lose touch.

Today's researchers have genealogy programs to help them sort through the family names of possible connections, and as we saw in Chapter 9, such connections are often the proof you need to establish family links.

Marriage Then Birth

1753 Hardwicke's Marriage Act is passed to prevent clandestine marriages (in England and Wales). It required parental permission if the man or woman was under the age of 21.

1823 The Marriage Act declared marriages without banns or licence valid, but the officiating minister a felon.

1837 1 July, the Births and Deaths Registration Act and the Marriage Act, both passed in 1836 (in England), come into force.

Until 1823 in England, and of course in her colonies, a man or woman under the age of 21 could not marry without parental consent. This explains the number of romantic (or otherwise) clandestine elopements both in novels and newspaper reports. After 1823, a boy was able to marry without permission at the age of 14, and a girl had to be 12, although "marriages at these ages were virtually unknown."[4] Only by the Marriage Act of 1929 was the legal age raised to 16 for both genders.

By then, of course, many colonies had become self-governing dominions and made their own laws, which vary with time and place. Throughout the 1880s and 1890s, Britain enacted a number of minor marriage laws to regularize certain situations. One of the most controversial, "marriage to deceased wife's sister," became an easy joke for Gilbert and Sullivan.

My niece, who was reading *Sense and Sensibility*, once asked me, "In those days would parents have approved of their daughter of 17 marrying a man 20 years older than she was?"

The answer is, "Of course they would approve. He was established and could support a family. She would have a comfortable life with him, and if she survived childbirth, might find herself at 30 a rich widow." That was true in Chaucer's day, in Jane Austen's time, and even now, young and pretty wives are not unheard of. And yes, you will find wealthy older women marrying much younger men: Chaucer's Wif of Bathe did.

- A young wife might find herself a rich widow, but only if she survived childbirth. That would determine her fate, for in 1870 "the risk of dying in childbirth was about 1 in 200."[5]

- The absence of effective birth control other than that provided by breast-feeding meant that if a loving husband exercised his marital rights, a wife, particularly if she employed a wet-nurse as most of the upper classes did, might be constantly pregnant.

     An Example: Between 1748 and 1778, Lady Emily (Lennox) Fitzgerald Ogilvy, Duchess of Leinster (1731–1814), bore 21 children, 19 Fitzgeralds (nine of whom died before they were 20), and two Ogilvy daughters by her second husband. Charles Dickens' wife had 10 children in 13 years, and Queen Victoria bore nine children between 1840 and 1857. The second Earl Grey (of tea fame) had 13 children by his wife and a daughter by the Duchess of Devonshire.

Children of the Mist

While "baby planting" was not unheard of,[6] most children's mothers, even if duchesses, are known. Paternity is quite another matter. Consider for a moment all the "children of the mist," as Pamela Fitzgerald once called them.[7] She herself was of uncertain parentage, rumoured to be the daughter of Madame de Genlis and the Duc d'Orleans. Modern biographers delight in sorting out who fathered whose children among the aristocracy. "If, as was widely supposed, William Lamb was Lord Egremont's son, and, as has been suggested, Caro [Lady Caroline Ponsonby] was fathered by Charles Wyndham — Egremont's third son — then Caro was marrying her uncle."[8]

Lucy Dillon, Marquise de La Tour du Pin, has a warning for researchers: "When society is so corrupt that corruption itself seems natural, and when no one is shocked at anything, why should anyone be astonished at excesses among the lower classes, who have been set such a bad example?"[9]

It does make one doubt Burke's and Debrett's pedigrees, though, and fear that one may find cuckoos in the nests of lesser folk as well. Nor were things much different a century later. Describing the weekend house parties at British stately homes in 1911 as "a heaven-sent opportunity for sex," Juliet Nicolson recounts several affairs of the famous that came to light including Sir Thomas Beecham and Lady Cunard.[10]

Divorce

Divorce was possible: Sir Charles Bunbury, for example, divorced Lady Sarah Lennox, the Duchess of Leinster's sister, in 1776. However it was very expensive. "Except in cases of annulment (on the grounds of non-consummation, for instance), which were dealt with by the ecclesiastical courts, divorce could only be secured by a private Act of Parliament and cost hundreds of pounds."[11]

In 1857, Parliament "took divorce and probate matters away from church courts and gave them, respectively, to new civil courts of divorce and probate."[12] Divorce then became possible, but "the number of marriages which ended in divorce was still under 500 a year in 1900."[13] Divorce was always legal in some Canadian provinces, and after 1930 in all but Quebec, where it still required an act of the Federal Parliament. Even so, it was still thought rather scandalous in the 1940s.

Birth Control

This was another taboo subject, although Margaret Sanger (1883–1966), a trained nurse, founded the first American birth-control clinic in Brooklyn in 1916. She was imprisoned for it, but after a world tour she founded the American Birth Control League in 1921.

- "Canadian pre-war [Second World War] society ... was a period of sexual repression ... when premarital sex was frowned on by the law, by the church and by society. The human body was not to be seen, fan dancers were jailed and the law demanded that men wear tops to their bathing suits.... The sale of contraceptives was a crime."[14]

- That society was also hypocritical. "Many movies of the thirties were, quite frankly, erotic.... Photography magazines pushed their artistic licence as far as possible to print the most revealing nude studies. Contraceptives were bootlegged under the counters of drugstore."

- Moral values and attitudes changed during the Second World War when a lot of young men "were thrust into a new society which was predominantly male, a military society in which they were at least permitted to talk about sex amongst themselves" and "they found that contraceptives [condoms] were an item of military issue."[15]

The above quotes are from the foreword "Without Approbation," written by Squadron Leader Bob Godfrey, R.C.A.F. (Ret'd) for Anthony Hopkins' *Songs from the Front and Rear: Canadian Servicemen's Songs of the Second World War*. The book, we are warned, is "**NOT** MEANT FOR CHILDREN," but the text that introduces each song will tell you more about life and death during that war, and other wars as well, than many more formal sources. The songs are rude, and funny too.

Death and Mourning

Until well into the twentieth century, child mortality was high; highest in large cities where poor sanitation and crowded conditions encouraged epidemics of diseases rarely encountered today. The death of children is always sad, but until recent medical advances in immunology, it was no stranger to our ancestors. The death of parents left many surviving children orphans as well.

- Funerals were important social events in most communities. Everyone dressed in black (or white, if the deceased was a child or young unmarried girl), and church bells would toll the death knell to let the parish know the deceased had been laid to rest.

- Consult any nineteenth century etiquette book. Proper funeral procedures were very elaborate in Victorian times, but, by 1932, Gertrude Pringle would write, "A great many feel that there should be drastic reforms in funerals on the side of greater simplicity and a reduction in the costs."[16]

- Etiquette books also give the required forms and times for wearing mourning for various family members. For women, full mourning meant all black clothing; it had to be dull black and worn with jet jewellery. After the first year, a widow could add touches of white and assume half-mourning. Parents and children were mourned for a year; grandparents, brothers, and sisters for six months, while three months sufficed for uncles and aunts. In-laws were mourned, as well, but for lesser times. First cousins got six weeks — but if there were 50 of them, it was probably best to have a wardrobe of black garments at the ready.

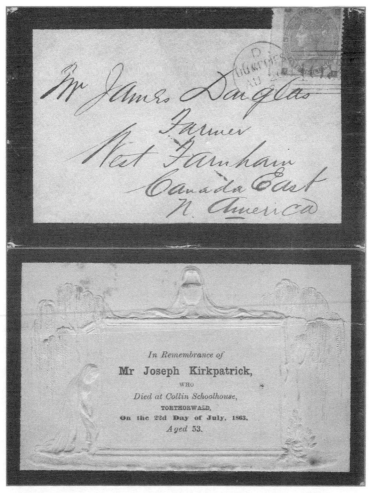

"The Letter Edged in Black." An envelope with a black border announced a death. Mourning cards would be sent to family and friends to tell the sad news.

- By 1932, we are told, "Deep mourning is now worn only for very close relatives, the tendency being to wear less heavy mourning and for shorter periods than formerly."[17] By this time, the widow's bonnet and heavy veil was being replaced by a black-veiled hat. I should add that, in 1932, whenever a lady left her house, she wore a hat and gloves.

Even for young women who still wore short skirts and had not yet "put up their hair," hats and gloves were always worn.

- In 1932, some women were working: "when a widow must mingle in the business world, she will find it advisable to curtail the period of mourning and forego the wearing of a black veil. Heavy mourning is out of place in an office, and is really the garb of a recluse."[18]

You can learn more about funeral and burial practices in *A Better Place: Death and Burial in Nineteenth Century Ontario* by Susan Smart (Toronto: Dundurn Press, 2011).

Chapter 11

Home Sweet Home

Tenements or Joint Occupancy

When we go looking for ancestors in the past, we need to understand how our housing patterns have changed, or haven't — as the case may be. A one-family house on a separate lot was the post–Second World War suburban ideal, but it was perhaps only a dream for many. Joint occupancy has always been how most people lived.

Historically, several generations often lived together, with children caring for ageing parents, or grandparents looking after the next generation. Maiden aunts and bachelor uncles might also be part of the family team; it took a lot of labour to keep a home and farm functioning, and everyone fed and clothed.

In cities, whether in Babylon, Caesar's Rome, medieval Paris, or nineteenth-century Brooklyn, the most common residences were large buildings housing a number of families. They used to be called tenements.

> Tenement — ... in large cities, tenement
> houses are buildings occupied by sev-
> eral families living independently of one
> another, but having a common right in the
> hall, staircases and outhouses.[1]

Apartment buildings still have halls and stairs, but out-
houses are no longer acceptable in an urban setting. Today,
we expect even the smallest apartment to have running
water and an indoor toilet.

The 1911 eleventh edition of *Encyclopædia Britannica*
continues, "In the heart of great towns the problem of
housing is a difficult one ..." and goes on to deplore "the
unsuitable and insanitary condition of many houses occupied in the tenement system." This was a serious problem,
and the encyclopedia entry on "housing" tells us that it had
been recognized as such for over 70 years, which is to say,
since the cholera epidemics of the 1830s and 1840s. These
forced local authorities to gradually accept the idea that
sanitation was linked to public health.[2] Improving conditions took until well into the next century.

Flats and Apartments

"Tenement" has a derogatory connotation. "A flat" or "an
apartment" can place the occupant anywhere in the social
scale, depending on how big the residence is and where
it is located. Essentially a flat usually means one floor of
a larger building, whereas there may be more than one
apartment (or tenement) to a floor. Flats and apartments
can be in buildings designed as multiple residences or in
houses converted into two or more dwelling spaces.

The bank in Sutton, Quebec. Commonly one of the most imposing buildings in a small town, most banks had a residence on the second floor for one of the senior employees, largely as a matter of security.

In Paris, as well as in many other European cities, eighteenth-century houses were usually four to six storeys. Merchants and their boutiques occupied the street level, and, in the age before the elevator, rents were lower on higher floors. Being "up one flight" was for the rich, agreeably removed from the bustle and noise of the street with large rooms and large windows. "Up two flights" was perfectly respectable, though the rooms might be less grand; "up three flights" was something to gloss over when describing your home. Above that you were in the garrets with labourers and the poor who crammed many more people into fewer and smaller rooms.

An Example: When Fanny Burney and her husband, General d'Arblay, were living in Paris in 1802, their lodging was in the Hotel Marengo, 1185 rue de Miromésnil, where, as she writes to her father, they had "a very pretty apartment ... up 3 pairs of stairs, to be sure — but *The nearer the Gods*, you know!" Writing to a friend at court however, she says they are "up two pairs of stairs" and describes a "neat Drawing room, a small ante-room which we make our Dining Parlour, a tidy Bed Chamber, & a closet within it for Alexander [her son]. This with a kitchen and a bit of a bedroom for my maid, all on the same floor.... "[3]

When Baron Haussmann rebuilt Paris in the third quarter of the nineteenth century he did little to change this pattern.[4] In London and New York, townhouses (the polite term for row housing) were more common than apartments. Row housing could be a small, squalid, two-up two-down slum dwellings, an elegant Georgian mansion in Mayfair, or a five-storey brownstone on Washington Square.

Now, most are sub-divided into a basement or garden flat, first and second floor flats, and perhaps a small attic flat. In North American cities there are variants of the town house.

- The double house has two two-storied residences, each having their own entrance but sharing a middle wall.

- The "duplex," on the other hand, may look like a single home but is built as upper and lower flats which may or may not share an entrance.

- A "triplex" consists of three flats stacked one above the other. In Montreal, many such buildings have an outdoor staircase curving up to the second floor.

- Then there is the "quadruplex," or double duplex. Any more than that and you live in an apartment house.

- Apartments can range from minuscule to the equivalent of a mansion with all the expected rooms, a separate library, and even a ballroom.

Dormitories, Bunkhouses, and Residences

Until the early twentieth century, some form of housing was often a condition of employment — and not only for domestic help. In fact, many businesses still establish "company towns" if they are exploiting the resources of a remote region, but there were other ways to provide room and board.

- Among a family's listing in census returns, you sometimes see the note, "In Shanty." It reminds us that lumber camps housed and fed the men who left their farms every winter to work in the woods.

- Mills and other water-powered nineteenth-century industries tended to be located where the power sources were, which weren't necessarily in centres of population, so owners often provided dormitories for their young, unmarried workers, the sexes strictly segregated of course.

- Large shops in Victorian cities occasionally housed their clerks in top-floor garrets. Dormitory living, however, was probably never all that popular, and by the turn of the century young, single workers wanted greater independence. See Rooms and Boarding Houses below.

- One of the few professions open to women was nursing; nurses were employed on both day and night shifts, so hospitals had to provide residential accommodation. So did teachers' colleges; and, once women were admitted to universities, these too had to provide separate, chaperoned residences.

- A very different group residence was the local poor house, usually a largish tenement where the local authorities housed the unfortunate, and often indigent, individuals or families of the town.

- Religious institutions ran orphanages and asylums, as well as their associated convents, monasteries, and seminaries. Residences for senior citizens are a more recent development, the result of much longer life expectancy. In earlier times the poor house usually took in the elderly.

Rooms and Boarding Houses

Leaving the country to make your fortune in the city is an old and familiar theme of folk tales and ballads. The growing population in the late nineteenth century brought more and more people to cities. Young bank clerks, or single teachers (male or female), as well as an increasing number office workers and store clerks, all had to find somewhere respectable to live. In a town where they had no relatives or family friends, a boarding house was often the only choice. Young married couples could also be found boarding, or in "rooms," before they had children and required a fully equipped home. Boarding houses came in a variety of types.

- A family with a spare bedroom or two could rent them out for the extra money This persists in tourist regions. We call them bed and breakfasts.

- One or two enterprising women might rent or buy a big house and make their living operating a larger boarding house.

- A widow, left with a big house, could add to her income by taking in boarders. If she had daughters, the young women could meet a whole series of available young men.

Quality and standards of accommodation — and guests — varied widely. Quiet, church-going boarders who didn't stay out late were usually preferred. Boarding-houses would often be segregated (all women or all men), but a mixture of sexes was not unusual. A room almost always came with breakfast; lunch was rare, and other meals were negotiable, but often not included if there were places to eat nearby.

Guests often lived in these houses for five days a week; many working girls and boys from the country went home by train on the weekend. As noted in Chapter 9, the men who ran those trains were frequently based in one town, but spent some nights at the other end of their run. The railways provided some dormitories or bunkhouses, but many stayed in boarding houses close to the train yards.

Then There Were Hotels

Most towns once had an inn where the stagecoach stopped. If it was near the train station, it became the railway hotel and served the wealthier travellers. These could include commercial travellers who went by train from town to town on a regular schedule, as well as some train conductors. Small town hotels counted on such regulars, and were happy to house bank clerks and teachers who wanted more than a boarding house offered.

Luxury Residential Hotels

Railway hotels with regulars were one thing, but in the large cities there were also very elegant residential hotels.

The Linton (built 1906–07) brought a new degree of service and comfort to Montreal, offering a ground-floor café, "which will easily accommodate one hundred and fifty guests," with a "ladies' entrance" on Simpson Street and a "ladies' tea-room" reserved for tenants and their guests. As in the New York apartment hotels, some of the units had no kitchen.[5]

If residents had a guest, there were individual rooms with baths that could be rented at need. The Sylvia Hotel in Vancouver also started life as this type of apartment hotel, with public rooms for entertaining, restaurants where guests could dine, room service for other meals, and usually laundry and valet service. For a wealthy couple, renting two or three serviced rooms with their own bath and, sometimes, a small kitchen, freed them from the "servant problem." Many hotels had servants' rooms, either on a low, noisy floor, or under the eaves, for a lady's maid or valet. Many of our recently built retirement residences offer amenities that are very similar to the once popular residential hotels.

Chapter 12

How We Lived Then

Having considered *where* people lived, it might be helpful to remember *how* they lived. Chapter 1 outlined how industry, transportation, and communication changed during the nineteenth and twentieth centuries. However, there are also many little things we take for granted, as well as amenities we expect will be there when we want them but rarely think about until they aren't available.

As you voyage back in time, you will reach a point when there were no switches to turn on lights, and then no matches to light candles, but you are unlikely to trace your family back to a time before candles.

Visual Records

Early man recorded his hunting exploits on cave walls. Seventeenth- and eighteenth-century aristocrats, as well as wealthy merchants, often had portraits painted of their families, houses, horses, or estates. In fact, we have quite an extensive visual record of human history as drawn, painted, and sketched by artists. Today, of course, visual images of our world surround us; we must remind ourselves that it was only in the 1840s that photography in its very early forms became available.

- Early photography required long exposures, so many photographers took pictures of places and buildings, which were stationary, in preference to people, who often moved too much. High-speed negatives (1/25 second) come along in 1878.

The daughters of Alonzo Todd; photographed in 1872, when long exposure times demanded rigid poses.

- By the mid-1850s, you can hope to find photographic portraits (mostly tintypes) of your ancestors. By the 1870s, expect to find cabinet photographs taken by commercial photographers; and by 1900, you will find black-page albums, often with out-of-focus snapshots taken by family members.

A Few Dates

1840 Commercial portrait *Daguerreotypes* date from this year.

1841 Talbot patented the calotype, the first photographs printed from a negative.

1854 Commercial *ambrotypes* (on glass) and *Cartes-de-visite* (on card) became available.

1856 Tintype patented, taking over the portable portrait market.

1866 Cabinet Photograph, 5.5 x 4 inches on card 6.5 x 4.5 inches, introduced.

1888 *Kodak* camera introduced by Eastman.

1890 Eastman introduced celluloid roll film, 35 millimetres.

1895 Auguste and Louis Lumière obtain French patents for combination motion picture camera, projector, and printer: *Cinématographe*. By 28 December moving pictures are being shown to a paying audience.

1900 First *Brownie* camera ushers in the age of snapshots.

1928 16 millimetres Kodacolor motion picture film introduced.

Old family photographs can remind us of earlier customs. The Douglas children seen here, probably in the summer of 1892, when the only boy, Cedric, was still "in petticoats," which is to say, still wearing diapers.

Civilization Is Running Water

Let's consider modern conveniences. Today, we depend on electricity for everything, even the basics: it provides light, heat, refrigeration, and pumps water. Running water is probably one of the greatest conveniences, but it is far from "modern."

- Water runs downhill, and in some places it's possible to find a spring on a hillside higher than where the water is needed. In fact, the ancient Romans constructed aqueduct systems to supply water to entire cities using gravity. My husband's great-grandfather laid a pipe from a hillside spring to bring water to taps in his farmhouse and barn.

- Engineers and inventors have been making water "flow uphill" for centuries using all sorts of ingenious devices.[1] Steam-powered pumps played a role in the industrial revolution, and today, in many parts of the world, a well with a hand pump is a welcome convenience. These were the source of most water in most cities well into the nineteenth century.

- A cottage my family once owned in New Brunswick had a hundred-gallon tank in the barn, with a well and a powerful hand-operated pump. The tank was mounted just under the roof, well above the ground floor of the house. Older children (and sometimes their friends) had the daily chore of pumping the tank full. You quickly learned to be very careful with water: no tap ever dripped in that house.

- A device that is less dependent on child labour is the hydraulic ram, an "automatic pump in which the kinetic energy of a descending column of water raises some of the water above its original level."[2] I learned about this at a friend's family home where they had one in a nearby brook. All I can report is that there was running water in the house, and the ram thumped in the distance day and night.

Heat and Cold

Fire keeps us warm and cooks our food; ice cools us and our food.

> **Heat**: hot air rises, and hot-air heating was used by the Greeks. There were other ancient civilizations who also heated their homes by circulating hot water under tiled floors.

- Wood and charcoal were the common fuels in the ancient world, though the Romans did use a little coal, particularly in Britain. Humans still use all three fuels, employing the same basic methods. Inventors may modify, and sometimes improve, the design of fireplaces and stoves, but we handle domestic fire much as our ancestors did.

- Gas and electricity came on the urban scene in the latter half of the nineteenth century; a gas flame is still fire and is treated as such. Electricity causes a coiled wire to give off heat and it can start a fire so must be used with the same caution as fire.

Match or Tinder Box

Spontaneous combustion is known to happen and lightning can strike a tree and start a forest fire, but neither of these accidents is a handy way to start a fire in a fireplace, much less light a candle, lamp, or cigarette. From the late nineteenth century to the present, this has been done by striking a match, holding it to the candle or lamp wick, or in the stove or fireplace using some paper and kindling, and perhaps blowing a little air to get it started. Today you can get wooden "strike anywhere" matches and safety matches, which must be struck on a special strip on the box or folder. Match folders used to be given away by hotels and restaurants, and were often specially printed for weddings and other events.

The elegant cigarette lighters you see being used in *Mad Men*, as well as in Noel Coward plays, use an older principle for creating fire: striking a flint with steel so that the spark lights a wick impregnated with a flammable fuel with which the lighter is filled.

Until "the beginning of the nineteenth century flint and steel with tinder box and sulphur-tipped splints of wood — 'spunks' or matches — were the common means of obtaining fire for domestic and other purposes."[3] Tinder was anything flammable, such as charred wood shavings, cotton lint, or some such mix that would catch fire from a spark, smoulder with enough heat to light the sulphur tip of the spunk, match, or spill, with which one lit the lamp or candle.

> The first really practical friction matches were made in England in 1827 by John Walker, a druggist of Stockton-on-Tees. These were known as "Congreves" ... and consisted of wooden splints or sticks of cardboard coated with sulphur and tipped with a mixture of chlorate of potash, sulphide of antimony, and gum.[4]
>
> The method of striking to obtain fire was to draw the splinter of wood tipped with this composition, rapidly and under considerable pressure, through a piece of folded sandpaper. These were imitated and named "Lucifers." None were easy to ignite.[5]

Not until 1833 was the phosphorus friction match introduced commercially in Austria and Germany. Unfortunately, the principle ingredient, yellow phosphorus, is a deadly poison and the fumes caused a particularly unpleasant disease among the workers who made the matches. By 1906, when an international convention banned yellow phosphorus, a wooden match made without it was available worldwide.

Ice and Cold

In ancient Rome, in eighteenth century England, and in 1930s North America, ice was cut from frozen ponds or glaciers and stored in insulated, sawdust-filled ice-houses until needed.

- Even in the 1930s, many homes and most cottages and camps had an icebox. The upper section held a large cake of ice that slowly melted, cooling air that sank down to the lower space where there were shelves for storing food. An iceman delivered new cakes of ice regularly.

- In rural Canada and the northern United States, ice was usually cut from ponds in the winter, and stored and distributed by the pond's owner. Where a larger population had to be served, this old technology was not sufficient. Ice had to be made, but how?

- In 1862, Dr. A. Kirk invented a coal-powered cooling machine that successfully made ice, about four pounds of ice per one pound of coal.

- A variety of economically efficient ice-making and cooling machines were developed over the next three decades. Making ice to sell in large cities was one priority. Another was to cool large spaces for the transportation or storage of perishable food, often as cold-storage rooms on a ship that, since it ran on coal anyhow, could use some for cooling.

- Electricity domesticated refrigeration, as it had with so many other things. The first

electric refrigerators were being manu-
factured on a large scale in America and
France by 1917.[6]

Let There Be Light

The house I stayed in with the hydraulic ram didn't have
electricity. Their stove and refrigerator ran on propane gas,
and they had an enviable collection of Victorian oil lamps
that actually burned kerosene.

- It was at that house that I learned that those
  picturesque lamps have to be gathered up
  each morning, brought to the kitchen,
  refilled, the wicks trimmed, and the glass
  chimneys washed clean of soot, then
  returned to their places.

- This type of lamp used whale oil until
  the early 1850s, when the Canadian Dr.
  Abraham Gesner discovered a method
  of extracting liquid fuel, which he called
  kerosene, from coal. In 1859, petroleum,
  from which kerosene can be distilled, was
  discovered. Cleaner and cheaper, it quickly
  replaced whale oil.

- The Phoenicians invented candles, and
  we have been using them for centuries.
  They give less light than oil lamps, and
  their maintenance is not quite as labour-
  intensive — unless of course you are making them yourself from tallow, wax, or the
  very expensive beeswax.

- Gas was first used for lighting city streets in London on one side of Pall Mall in 1807, then in 1810 in Westminster; Baltimore followed in 1816, Paris in 1819, and Berlin in 1826. It took almost half a century for gas lighting to be accepted in urban homes, only to be replaced by electric lights in the years between the two world wars.

- Electric arc-lamps were installed in a Parisian department store in 1877; they were very bright and used direct current. They were more successfully used in light-houses, and at one time were the spotlights in most theatres, but they were not suitable for domestic use.

- Both gas and electricity are delivered to houses through either a pipe or a wire. This works fine in urban settings, where many homes are close together and a central generating station can supply a lot of cus-tomers, making the service economically viable.

- In isolated places, gasoline-powered gen-erators can provide electricity in an emer-gency; propane gas is available in small and large pressurised tanks. However, both are expensive forms of energy. Windmills are a much older power source, but depend on wind, which is a variable and uncontrol-lable element.

Electric Lights — Not Before 1879

That was the year Thomas Alva Edison patented his carbon filament light bulb in the U.S. and Sir Joseph Swann produced a similar one in England.

- In 1881, Godalming in Surrey, England, became the first town in the world to have electricity for public and private usage, as part of a three-year experiment (a few private schemes were inaugurated a little earlier), after which the town reverted to gas lighting. The electricity supply was generated first by water-power, then by a steam engine.[7]

- In 1934, the "use of electricity is so common in Canada that it is difficult to conceive of using any other means of lighting the homes, stores, factories and streets in urban municipalities."[8]

- It took longer to electrify rural Canada. That same 1934 report assured readers that "the service is being extended rapidly to rural areas."[9] That is "government-speak," but after the Second World War, rural electrification reached most of Canada, though in the country it was always wise to have a box of candles and two or three lamps full of kerosene in case the power line went down in a storm. It still is a wise precaution.

Labour-Saving Appliances

Some would-be wit once said that the best labour-saving device is a competent servant. A decade or two into the nineteenth century, a widow with an annual income of £400 would normally have a live-in servant. Lord Durham, jogging on with one hundred times that income, probably expected to pay well over a hundred servants to run Lambton Castle. In 1895, some two-million servants were employed in the homes of the British upper-classes.

However, as the century progressed and new fields of work opened up, the next generation was unwilling to continue in service. "The number of servants registered on the National Census in 1911 was a fifth lower than in 1891."[10] In part, this was because technical advances made many tasks obsolete, such as trimming and filling lamps, or carrying water to the upstairs bedrooms.

This was particularly true in North America, where housewives had always relied less on domestic help and were glad to have the mechanical assistance of a hand-cranked apple peeler or a lever-operated clothes washer. Labour-saving devices powered by newly available electricity were conceived in the nineteenth century, but grew up early in the twentieth. Most were motorized versions of hand or foot-powered mechanical devices that already existed.

The commercial development of the necessary electric motor depended on the general acceptance of alternating-current electricity, rather than the direct current Thomas Edison favoured for domestic use. It was the Croatian-born Nikola Tesla, who emigrated to the United States in 1884, and the American-born George Westinghouse whom we have to thank.

1883 Nikola Tesla built the first alternating-current (AC) induction motor.

1889 Nikola Tesla patented an efficient multiple-phase electric motor; two years later, in association with George Westinghouse, he produced a small portable fan.[11] The electric fan's ability to move air has changed the way we heat and cool many of our homes.

1889 Isaac Singer saw the potential of electricity to power small machines and introduced an electrically powered model of his sewing machine. The treadle-operated machine remained in use in Toronto schools even in the 1930, and is still used today in many developing countries.

1893 The Chicago World's Fair was illuminated by electricity using Westinghouse alternating current based on Tesla's patents. A model kitchen on display showed an electric stove, electric fans, and an automatic dishwasher.

By the end of the First World War, many middle-class women in North America did a good part of their own housework and could fully appreciate the benefits of labour-saving electric devices. They also had enough disposable income to buy them. The coincidence of these factors explains the rapidity with which the American home altered in the early 1900s.[12]

Electric irons were the most widely owned appliance; by 1927 three-quarters of the electrified homes in the United States had one, since they were a lot easier, and cooler, than heating heavy flat-irons on wood stoves. To learn more about how many modern conveniences developed, consult Witold Rybczynski's *Home: A Short History of an Idea*. The idea he refers to is that home should be comfortable. The book is filled with interesting facts and information, some of which I have scattered through this book.

Food — Both Fast and Slow

1762 John Montagu, the fourth Earl of Sandwich, ordered what would become the first sandwich (meat between two slices of buttered bread) during a 24-hour gaming session.

1837 Pharmacists John Lee and William Perrins concocted Worcestershire Sauce, a fermented condiment flavoured with anchovies, tamarind extract, onions, garlic, and spices. It became a milestone in British cuisine.

1930 The *Daily Mirror* reported that "in the North of England, bread is being sold sliced and wrapped."[13] Pre-sliced bread was an idea imported from North America, where the convenience food had been available since 1925.

In the fall of 1980, my husband and I attended a conference in Bulgaria, which was still behind the Iron

Time Traveller's Handbook

Curtain at the time. It was like stepping back in time to the early 1930s, particularly as regards the food served in the deluxe hotel dining room. Bulgaria was then desperately short of hard currency, and didn't waste it on importing out of season lettuce or fresh oranges. We ate what was in season, and largely what was grown locally. (Today, we call it the "hundred-mile diet," which has become quite trendy.) Veal, tomatoes, cucumbers, and peppers both green and red, were on the menu for every meal, breakfast included. Apricot nectar was the standard juice at breakfast, but one morning, to everyone's excitement, the buffet boasted several large tins of grapefruit juice imported from Cuba.

That table also had a single electric toaster, slow and unreliable, on which guests could make toast. Even untoasted, the bread was very good, there was unsalted butter, lots of fruit jams, and several flavours of yogourt. We ate well, but the menu was monotonous. It would have been different at other times of the year, but equally repetitive day to day.

Back at home, that fall of 1980, I had a vast choice of fruit and vegetables from warmer climates, even in the dead of winter. I could buy frozen lamb from New Zealand (fresh in late winter), as well as fresh fish from around the world. However, I grew up during the Great Depression, and in winter in the 1930s and 1940s, we ate root vegetables and apples. Peas, green beans, corn, peaches, and pears came in cans; so did salmon. For fish on Friday there was also finnan haddie (smoked haddock) or dried salt cod.

A recipe for salt cod: "Pick apart ½ a pound
of salt codfish. Wash it thoroughly in two

waters. Soak it overnight in cold water. Next morning, drain, cover with boiling water, and cook below the boiling point for five minutes. Drain and press."[14]

This was served with plain, boiled potatoes, hard-boiled eggs sliced into cream sauce, and tinned peas. Mother made sure we had cod, potatoes, and sauce left over. Mash the potatoes, flake the cod into fine pieces, mix together with the sauce, and form into cakes; roll the cakes in dry bread crumbs and fry in butter, serve for lunch on Saturday or Sunday breakfast.

In Toronto and Montreal in those pre-war years, you could buy pineapples that came from Hawaii by boat, ripening en route. Bananas from Central America or the Caribbean did the same, while grapefruit and oranges came by train from Florida. Asparagus, hot-house tomatoes, and "out of season" strawberries were grown "in the States," but they were very expensive luxuries few could afford. Rural families could grow their own vegetables, and many urban residents had friends or family with large gardens.

- My husband's parents lived in the country and had a vegetable garden. They grew their potatoes, dug them in the fall, and stored them in the basement where they developed a tangle of sprouts over the winter. Turnips were waxed, and carrots and parsnips were kept in a pit in the garden insulated by straw.

- Eggs, often the small and cheaper pullet's eggs that were available in the fall, were "put down" in water glass (sodium or potassium silicate and water) in five-gallon earthenware crocks. The same size crocks held the well-salted butter that was also kept in cold, but not freezing, earth-floored, basement storerooms.

- Tomatoes and green beans were "put down" in glass jars, a hot and tedious late-summer chore, just as making fruit and berry jams and preserves were in July. Making pickles and crab-apple jelly were September chores, but they added variety to winter meals.

- In towns and cities there were butchers, but electric refrigerators meant there was no need to shop for food every day. In both Montreal and Toronto we had a milkman and a breadman who made daily deliveries. The laundryman came twice a week.

- At our cottage in the country, the farmer up the road brought us milk daily, a fisherman arrived at the crack of dawn on Fridays with fresh-caught mackerel, and once a week a local farmer came round with lamb in the trunk of his car. You could buy a front quarter, a rear quarter, or even a section of ribs. He used a hatchet to separate the chops. The rest of the butchering was your problem.

- The milk we had delivered was unpasteurized, and there was a week or two in July when it tasted horribly of buttercups.

- A third farmer brought 'round in-season, fresh vegetables. We never thought about pesticides; you used Paris Green to kill potato bugs, and the fertilizer was either horse or cow manure. Sometimes fields were spread with lobster shells, and the gulls had a great time.

- The only frozen food in my youth was ice cream. As kids, we would follow the ice-man's wagon to suck on the fallen chips of ice; or if there were a large chunk left by the road, rush it home and beg mother to make ice cream — "Yes, of course, we will all help turn the freezer crank." At Christmas, a turkey and a few partridges were left to freeze in my grandfather's barn. With luck, they would keep until the "January thaw." When that came they all had to be cooked and eaten very quickly.

The end of the Second World War changed many things in the kitchen, and it was not just the end of rationing:

- In 1948, the editor of the *Wise Encyclopedia of Cookery* was enthusiastic about a "new technique of cooking": the pressure cooker. The principle had been around since 1681, but once the war was over manufacturers were "competing in the race to bring better and cheaper cookers to the market."[15]

- In 1948, "Industry has come to realize almost over-night the advantages of the process known as 'quick-freezing' food."[16] Suddenly refrigerator freezing compartments had to hold more than two trays of ice cubes and two bricks of ice cream. Do you remember when ice cream came in the shape of a brick and was served by the slice?

- Improved transportation, by air and by truck, changed how and where food was grown, processed, and distributed. Shopping malls proliferated; as the local butchers, fishmongers, and greengrocers retired, they were not always replaced. Supermarkets grew larger and larger.

Pendulums swing, though. Today, an opposing reaction to large supermarkets has set in, and we are urged to eat locally grown produce, enjoy slow (home cooked) food again, and chic areas in cities boast an array of small shops housing local butchers, bakers, and organic greengrocers. Now, you're even expected to bring your own shopping bag, just as great-grandmother did.

The Right to Privacy

The right to privacy is a fairly recent popular concept. In the twenty-first century, we look back at the nineteenth and are amused by our ancestors' fixation on modesty, decorum, and proper behaviour. We often forget that they saw nothing wrong in listening in to neighbours' conversations on their new "party-line" telephones. Will our descendants look back with equal amusement at our era's obsession with privacy? It only became a politically fashionable cause in the 1980s.

If you were born after 1980, you are probably active on various social networks; unless you and your friends take great care, much of your private life is readily accessible. Probably more so than you think.

The 18 December 1999 issue of *The Economist* contained an article called "Living in the Global Goldfish Bowl."[17] Reading it, you may be appalled to discover how much the British investigator being interviewed could find out about the journalist. In 1999, a computer trail led from an electoral list to the journalist's telephone number and address, then to a business directory with biographical data, then to a birth registration, and with it the mother's maiden name, and so on into the man's financial records. It is quite a horror story if you have illusions of privacy, but informative if you too want to locate someone. Today, if anyone is fool enough to post personal information on the Internet, they deserve their fate.

Actually, more people can probably find out more about you than anyone knew about your ancestors — except, of course, for their relatives, friends, and neighbours. "What will Mrs. Grundy say? What will Mrs. Grundy think?" That line from the play *Speed-the-Plough*, written in 1798 by Tom Morton, reminds us that our ancestors, just like Morton's Mrs. Ashfield, were very concerned about what their neighbours might know and say of them. In 1798, by the way, anyone in any position of authority who might have been curious about someone's activities could have intercepted letters, just as some employers can monitor email today — only the technology has changed.

Chapter 13

Health in the Past

There was no influenza in my young days.
We called a cold a cold.[1]

Influenza, or the flu, still attacks regularly, whether in avian or porcine guise, unlike a variety of other infections that once afflicted us. In the 1970s, I worked in a Montreal hospital, and one day I overheard a young resident asking a senior surgeon, "What is diphtheria like? I've never seen a case." The surgeon replied to the effect of, "You belong to a very lucky generation." Then he told the young man about the acutely infectious bacterial disease that we now encounter primarily in Victorian novels.

As you travel back in time, you will come upon more and more diseases we rarely suffer from today, coupled with less and less understanding of their causes and treatments. In the nineteenth century, vaccination and other inoculations against common diseases were developed and improved. Before the Second World War, sulpha drugs, then penicillin, were new weapons against infections. By the 1970s, even in a large city like Montreal, it was perfectly possible that a young doctor would never encounter a case of what was once a frequent cause of death.

Common ailments you may come across in your time travels:

ague	recurring fever & chills, often indicative of malarial infection
apoplexy	a stroke
biliousness	jaundice, often associated with liver disease
colic	extreme intestinal pain often with abdominal bloating
corruption or mortification	infection
costiveness	constipation
croup	a disease of children, with hoarseness and trouble breathing, sometimes confused with diphtheria

dropsy	oedema (U.S. edema), swelling or watery fluid collecting in tissues, often caused by kidney or heart disease
dyspepsia	indigestion
falling sickness	epilepsy
ship fever, or camp/jail fever	typhus
lung fever	pneumonia
putrid fever	diphtheria or typhus
remitting fever	malaria
yellow jack	yellow fever
flux	abnormal discharge from the body
french pox	venereal disease
gout	painful inflammation of the smaller joints, usually the toes, caused by an excess of uric acid salts in the blood, often hereditary.

green sickness	iron deficiency, anemia
king's evil or scrofula	tubercular infection of the throat lymph glands
lumbago/sciatica	lower back pain or back, hip, and leg pain
palsy	paralysis
quinsy	acute tonsillitis
summer complaint	diarrhea, caused by spoiled food or milk, or by insects spreading bacteria from outhouses

If your ancestors had further medical complications, you can consult Elizabeth Briggs's book *A Family Historian's Guide to Illness, Disease & Death Certificates*, which is full of useful data.

A Chronology of Health

460 B.C.E.   Hippocrates (c.460–357 B.C.E.) doctrine of the four humours.

430 B.C.E.   Bubonic plague, Athens, first in recorded in history.

160	Galen (129–199), Greek physician, demonstrated that arteries carry blood, not air.
1303	Spectacles invented.
1334–1337	"Black Death" (bubonic plague) originating in China and Central Asia spreads to Middle East and Crusaders.
1348	Black Death sweeps across Europe.
1349	Black Death reaches England. Kills between one-third and one-half of the population in a matter of months.
1563	Bubonic plague in London.
1603	Plague in London.
1625	William Harvey (1578–1657) describes circulation of the blood.
1665	April, plague breaks out in London (Great Plague of London).
1666	Autumn, plague ends having killed over 100,000. (Note that the Great Fire of London occurred 2–6 September.)
1676	Antony van Leewenhock (1632–1723) observes small organisms

(germs) under his home-made microscope.

1729–1730   Influenza, originating in Russia, spreads across Europe and America.

1781   The Influenza pandemic sweeps both Europe and the Americas.

Cholera sickens over 500 British soldiers in Ganjam, India.

1796   Edward Jenner (1749–1823) pioneers vaccination against smallpox, injecting people with the milder form of cowpox.

1817–1820   Cholera, originating in India spreads across Asia from Turkey to Japan, but does not reach England.

1829–1851   Cholera, spreads from Bengal to Europe, Japan, and North America.

1831   October, William Sproat is the first death from cholera in England. Throughout the rest of the nineteenth and early twentieth century epidemics of cholera flare up every few years, especially in large cities where the population density was high and sanitation poor.

1842	First use of ether as anaesthetic by C. Long in the U.S.
1847	Montreal, ship fever (typhus) kills over 9,000 immigrants.
1854	On 8 September, the handle was removed from the public water pump in Broad Street, Soho, London, halting an outbreak of cholera. To learn more about cholera, consult Steven Johnson's *The Ghost Map*.
1857–1859	Worldwide influenza pandemic.
1860	Pasteurization technique developed by Louis Pasteur in France.
1863–64	Clinical thermometer introduced by W. Aitken in U.K.
1865	Germ theory of disease published by Pasteur in France.
1867	First antiseptic operation performed by J. Lister in U.K.
1885	Cholera bacillus identified by E. Koche in Germany.
1889–1890	"Russian flu" kills 250,000 in Europe, three-times that worldwide.
1892	Cholera, worldwide pandemic kills some two million.

1895	X-rays discovered by W. Röntgen in Germany.
1899	Protozoan transmitted by a mosquito identified as cause of malaria.
1900	Virus transmitted by mosquito identified as cause of yellow fever.
1901	Blood groups identified by K. Landsteiner in Austria.
1918	Spanish flu pandemic kills more people than the First World War, which had just ended.
1921	Insulin isolated by F. Banting and C. Best in Canada.
1928	Dr. Alexander Fleming (1881–1955) discovers effect of penicillin on bacteria.
1929	Iron lung designed by P. Drinker and C. McKhann in U.S.
1932	First sulphonamide developed by G. Domagk in Germany.
1937–1944	Vaccine against yellow fever developed, first for a human viral disease.
1940	Howard W. Florey and Ernst Chain isolate and purify penicillin, develop techniques for large-scale production, conduct first clinical trials.

1945	Fleming, Florey and Chain share Nobel Prize for medicine for their work on penicillin.
1948	World Health Organization (WHO) starts as agency of United Nations.
1950	First successful kidney transplant.
1953	F. Crick and J. Watson discover double helix of DNA.
1955	Salk anti-polio vaccine widely distributed.
	Ultrasound successfully used in body scanning by I. Donald in the U.K.
1957–1958	Asian flu epidemic, mortality rates are relatively low.
1960	Oral contraceptives marketed in U.S.
1961–1970	Cholera pandemic.
1967	First heart transplant performed by C. Barnard, South Africa.
1968-1969	Hong Kong flu kills some 700,000 worldwide.
1971	CAT (computerized axial tomographic) scanner developed in the U.K.
1978	First test-tube baby born in the U.K.

1983　　　HIV (human immunodeficiency virus) identified as related to AIDS.

1989–1990　Flu epidemic in the U.K. kills over 29,000 people.

1999–2003　West Nile Virus isolated in the U.S., some 4,300 cases, around 300 fatalities.

2002–2003　SARS starts in south China, spreads in South East Asia and Canada, 4,461 recorded cases, 251 deaths.

2008–2009　Swine Flu pandemic creates worldwide media hysteria.

Chapter 14

Our Heritage

The Lion and the Unicorn were fighting for the Crown
The Lion beat the Unicorn all round the town.
Some gave them white bread and some gave them brown,
Some gave them plum cake and drummed them out of town.[1]

The speed of change in the twenty-first century can make even the recent past seem alien. Looking back just a century, we encounter customs and practices we might find strange, undemocratic, or, if we are feeling kindly, quaint. Some of these derive from our colonial past, since the provinces and territories that make up Canada were first a part of the French colonial empire, then the British — those that were not owned by the Hudson's Bay Company.

In fact, most of what has been handed down to us from our past — be it language, social customs, parliament, or laws — are rooted in either British or French traditions.

We share these with many newcomers to Canada, many of whom come from countries that have similar colonial roots. Indeed, at one time most of us were British subjects.

Loyal British Subjects

Before 1 January 1947, people born in British North America (or Canada, after 30 June 1867), were all "natural born British subjects." Indeed, at that time if you could prove you were born within the British Empire you could claim full nationality rights as a British subject.

- When people emigrated to Canada from the British Isles, or those red spots on older maps, it was essentially an internal migration of British subjects. Few records were kept unless the individuals were part of some special subsidized group or settlement plan.

- On arrival, they were automatically citizens, with the rights and responsibilities that brought. Aliens (anyone not originally a British subject) had to be naturalized. Remember that Americans were "aliens."

After the Second World War, the British Empire was gradually dismantled to be replaced by the Commonwealth, which was formed in 1949 when eight countries — Australia, Britain, Canada, Ceylon (Sri Lanka), India, New Zealand, Pakistan, and South Africa — signed the Declaration of London after a six-day conference. In the short term not much changed; over the following decades everything did.

1947 1 January, Canadian Citizenship Act comes into force. However, Canadians could still claim to be British subjects at Heathrow immigration.

1948 British Nationality Act conferred the status of British citizen on all Commonwealth subjects, recognizing their right to work and settle in the U.K. and bring their families with them.

1971 British Immigration Act limited the "right of abode" to those with a prior link (parents or grandparents) to the U.K.

1973 Britain joins European Economic Community (EEC), later the European Union (EU), and British citizens become citizens of Europe.

1981 British Nationality Act, abolished the 1948 definition of British citizen, replacing it with three categories: British citizen, citizenship of British dependent territories, and British overseas citizen. Only British citizens had the right to live in the U.K. Canadians become foreigners at Heathrow immigration.

1987 The Single European Act means that by 1992 people of EU member states have the right to work and study in any EU country.

Today, British citizenship can be acquired by birth — if at the time of birth either parent is a British citizen settled in the U.K.; descent — for a person born abroad, if either parent is a British citizen at the time of birth; or naturalization — at the discretion of the Home Secretary.

Because of large post-war emigration from the U.K., many Canadians have one parent who was a British citizen when they were born. They qualify for a British passport, which now gives them access to the entire EU.

Not Before

As with technology, there is very often a date before which a person cannot be a citizen of a country because that country did not exist.

- None of my grandparents were born in Canada, although my family have all lived in the same small region of North America for four generations or more. I was born in Canada, as were my parents, but their parents were born before 1 July 1867. They were all born in New Brunswick, then a separate, self-governing British colony.

- My husband's family lived in the Eastern Townships for almost as long, and three of his grandparents were born in Canada. However, they were born in the Province of Canada, another self-governing British colony created on 10 February 1841 by the Act of Union that brought together the two colonies of Upper Canada and Lower Canada.

- My husband's fourth grandparent was born in Adirondak, in New York State, where her parents spent a few years during a mining boom. She was born in the United States, a country that has existed since the Treaty of Paris was signed on 3 September 1783.

- Many of our Loyalist ancestors, not to mention earlier settlers (planters), were not born in the United States. They were born in the individual British colonies that made up pre-revolutionary British North America.

- With American ancestors, be aware that while France had ceded the Louisiana Territory to Spain in 1762, it was returned to France in 1800 and sold to the United States of America in 1803. Florida was purchased from Spain in 1819. States in the southwest were taken from Mexico after the war of 1846–48. Alaska was bought from Russia in 1867, and Hawaii annexed in 1898.

- Acadians were expelled from Nova Scotia in 1755, most to British colonies along the Atlantic coast, but some to France. Much later, in 1785, Acadians were accepted by the Spanish in Louisiana.

- Acadians were allowed to return to Nova Scotia and settle after 16 July 1764, and slowly many did trickle back. The families that had ended up in France made up the bulk of the Acadians who went to Louisiana in 1785; however, there are many families in Poitou-Charente who proudly boast of Acadian ancestry.

- If your ancestors spoke Italian or German, your challenges will be similar. Until the late nineteenth century, Germany was not a country, but a collection of kingdoms, principalities, grand duchies, dukedoms, electorates, free cities, and a few large private estates, each with their own bureaucracy and laws, much like Italy. Italy had the Papal States as well.

- The same is true elsewhere in Europe, the Middle East, Asia, or Africa. Borders were drawn, wars fought, borders changed, treaties signed, and borders changed again. You will find that the exact dates and the precise changes to borders are essential facts you must have to locate a birthplace, determine citizenship, and find records. Historical atlases for any specific region can be helpful.

North America Was Different

French and British practices encountered difficulties when they were transferred to North America. In the old world, land meant wealth, and labour was readily available. In North America, in the early days of settlement, land was plentiful and available but covered in forest. Workmen willing to clear it for someone else were hard to find. Thus, depending on your social class, there were two conflicting notions.

- North Americans settlers expected to own their own land; in fact, they demanded it. They were quite prepared to clear land for a farm of their own, and after several generations they were very skilled at it. As settlements in the original colonies prospered and grew — and remember that fertility was high and infant mortality low — "the surplus population 'swarmed' and went off to found new communities and townships."[2] Young New England families accepted it as the norm. Boys grew up with an axe in their hand, helping fathers and uncles "chop."

- In Quebec, a seigneurial system of land ownership was established and run rather the way things were in France. After the conquest, British officials imagined this new land would be just like home, where they owned the land and respectful tenant farmers paid them an annual rent. For the few who acquired seigneuries in Canada, it did turn out this way.

- Elsewhere, even though some men of influence with dreams of grandeur secured large tracts of land, they found that respectful tenants willing to pay rent were few and far between. Nor were workmen always available to clear the land much to the dismay of land hungry upper-class immigrants.

Think of all those army officers on half-pay given a
military grant of 500 acres of wilderness, then finding out
that things didn't work the way they did in the old world.
This confused the social order, accounting for much of
the tension between the new-from-Britain arrivals and the
native-born "Americans." One such family of British gentry
left us a record. Three children of Thomas Strickland of
Reydon Hall in Suffolk came to Upper Canada: Samuel
(1804–1867) in 1825, followed in 1832 by his sisters
Susanna (1803–1885) wife of Lieutenant J.W.D. Moodie,
and Catherine Parr (1802–1899) married to Lieutenant
Thomas Traill, 21st Fusiliers. All published accounts of
their experiences.

- All three Stricklands are quoted frequently
  in Ryan Taylor and Frances Hoffman's
  Across the Waters, itself an invaluable source
  of information on nineteenth century
  travel to, and life in, Upper Canada.

- Mrs. Traill wrote *The Female Emigrant's
  Guide and Hints on Canadian Housekeeping*,
  first published in 1854 and reprinted the
  following year as *The Canadian Settler's
  Guide*. For time travellers who venture
  into the backwoods of the Canadas, it is
  a wonderful manual as it must have been
  to female settlers, advising them what to
  bring (sturdy clothing and lots of shoes),
  what to buy on arrival (household goods
  and implements that suit the country),
  how to graft apple trees, make fermenta-
  tions for bread (home-made yeast), roast

a black squirrel, brew spruce beer, what to substitute for tea and coffee — you name it, though she does admit to an ignorance of bee keeping.

- Travel 70 years farther back and you will find another remarkable guide. In *A Midwife's Tale: The Life of Martha Ballard, Based on Her Diary 1785-1812*, the historian Laurel T. Ulrich recreates and explains the life and society of an early settlement on the Kennebec River in Maine. It was made into a TV movie for PBS, and the film was shot at King's Landing, the historic village near Fredericton, New Brunswick. Martha Ballard's world is so typical of North American backwoods life, that it will fill you in on your Loyalist ancestors' struggles, from a woman's and a domestic point of view, which is rare indeed from those years.

- For an aristocratic Irish-French woman's views on how to run a farm in upstate New York in the 1790s, as well as life at the French Court before the Revolution and in Napoleon's Europe after, dip into *Memoirs of Madame de La Tour du Pin*. The 1913 edition was translated and abridged by Felice Harcourt, and although it reads like romantic fiction, every word is true.

- A study that will guide you back into rural Quebec is Allan Greer's *Peasant, Lord, and*

Merchant: Rural Society in Three Quebec Parishes 1740-1840. The study is based on surviving documents and examines three parishes on the lower Richelieu River to give us an interesting picture of a changing society. The archivist, Marianne McLean, has done a similar service in *The People of Glengarry*. It is essential reading if you originate there.

Faiths of Our Fathers

Hierarchical denominations like the Roman Catholic and Anglican (Episcopalian) churches view authority as descending from Heaven to pope or crown, thence to archbishop (archdiocese), bishop (diocese), then the individual parish priest or rector. Such a structure can manage a world-wide organization with many and varied individual sub-structures, but it is authoritarian in nature. Their great virtue is the production and preservation of excellent records.

In the Anglican Church, a rector might hold several livings (a position with an income or property, according to the *Canadian Oxford Dictionary*) and employ a vicar or curate to care for the lesser ones, allowing them a portion of the tithes. Tithes were the 10 percent of his produce that each farmer or tradesman paid yearly to the local parish clergyman or incumbent.

- The parish was also a unit of local government responsible to the local Justice of the Peace for relief of the poor, maintaining law and order, and other local services (see Courts of Quarter Session on page 233).

- Church and civil parishes might or might not have the same boundaries. Roman Catholic and Anglican churches existing in the same places rarely had the same parish boundaries.

- Canonical hours of prayer were of importance to religious orders and in earlier times were recognized by both the Roman Catholic and Anglican churches:

  1. Matin, the first service, originally at midnight, later combined with Laud as the first service of the day.

  1a. Laud

  2. Prime, at daybreak or 6.00 a.m.

  3. Tierce, third hour of the day, or 9.00 a.m.

  4. Sext, sixth hour, or noon

  5. Nones, ninth hour or 3.00 p.m.

  6. Vespers, late afternoon, Evensong (Church of Engand)

  7. Compline, the last service of the day after the evening meal, now often offered directly following Vespers.

Congregational denominations tended to be formed by dissenters, rebels against these established churches, developing structures where each congregation is responsible for its own activities but may join with other groups in some sort of co-operative assembly (Conference, Synod or Council) to manage affairs that go beyond the smaller unit.

In the seventeenth century, certain colonies in the New World attracted settlers from such congregations because they offered religious freedom. Such sects had a tendency to split over minor points of theology, and while their history is sprinkled with charismatic preachers and leaders, their records are only as good as the individual sect, minister, or congregation wanted them to be.

In What Became Canada

A wide variety of religious beliefs still flourish in Canadian cities, at least as many as you would find on a nineteenth-century census return. Today, those beliefs include most of the world's diverse religions; in the nineteenth-century they were almost all Christian. It was the Protestant congregations that provided the variety.

In the eighteenth century, people came to what is now Canada from both the American colonies and Great Britain, so our religious institutions evolved from both British and North American churches and sects. In the nineteenth century, the result is a confusing number of Protestant beliefs and churches. At the time of Confederation, one sometimes finds different branches of the same denomination as rivals in a town. The nineteenth century census returns give some idea of what can be found, but these will vary depending on which sects are common in a region.

No Denomination Categories: Atheist, Christian, Free Thinker, Independent, Not Given, Protestant.

Established Churches: Roman Catholic, Church of England (Anglican), which I once found spelled "Englican," Episcopal/Episcopalian (Anglican but via U.S.), Episcopal Church in Scotland (Anglican in Scotland), and on rare occasions the Church of Ireland (Anglican in Ireland).

Baptists might simply be Baptist, or else Christian Conference Baptist, Free Will Baptists, Reformed Baptist, Regular Baptist, Newlight Baptist, Primitive Baptists.

Methodist Churches: In addition to Methodist, and Wesleyan Methodist, there were British Episcopal Methodist, Calvinistic Methodist, Episcopal Methodists, Independent Methodist, New Connection Methodist, Primitive Methodist, and Reformed Methodist.

Presbyterians could be simply Presbyterian, but there were as well American Presbyterian, Canadian Presbyterian, Church/Kirk of Scotland, Free Church, Free Kirk, Reformed Presbyterian, United Presbyterian, and even Wesleyan Presbyterians. Cameronians are a small group that broke from the Church of Scotland, and were active in early Eastern Ontario settlements

Other Denominations: Adventist, Bible Believer, Bible Christian, Bretheren, Christian Brethren, Congregationalist, Church of Christ, Dunkard or Tunker, Deist, Jewish, Latter Day Saints, Lutheran, Mennonite, Quaker or Friend, Seventh Day Adventist, Unitarian, Universalist.

Only at the end of the nineteenth century and into the twentieth did many of these congregations merge and unite. In the *Historical Atlas III*, Plate 34, G.J. Matthews has drawn a pedigree chart illustrating "The Road to Church Union."[3] It shows how many local and regional Presbyterian synods had to join together to form the Presbyterian Church in Canada (1867), and is equally enlightening as to when and how Wesleyan Methodists, Methodist Episcopal Churches (U.S. and Canadian), Primitive Methodists, Bible Christians, and New Connexion Methodists slowly got together as the Methodist Church of Canada, Newfoundland & Bermuda in 1884.

The United Church of Canada

Researchers from other places may not be familiar with the United Church of Canada, an institution unique to this country. On 10 June 1925, "Church Union" amalgamated the Methodist Church of Canada, about half the Presbyterian churches, the Congregational Union, and the Union Churches of Western Canada into the United Church of Canada. In 1968, the Evangelical United Brethren Church joined. While the United Church of Canada Archives hold a lot of early church records, there is also a Presbyterian Church Archive and a lot of material in various regional repositories.

Courts of Quarter Session

Quarter sessions originate far back in the history of English jurisprudence, coming from a statute of 1388 that dictated that the justices shall keep their sessions in at least every quarter of the year. The quarter sessions are a local court of record, held by justices of the peace of any county — or any part, division, or city within a county — in general sessions assembled, and has both a limited criminal jurisdiction and some civil jurisdiction.

In the United Kingdom, the local aristocracy and landed gentry were the justices of the peace and carried out the court's decisions. In British North America, justices of the peace were appointed by the governor and council from among the educated and more prominent landowners and presided at the Courts of Quarter Session, which were the colonies' basic form of local government.

The courts not only dealt with petty crimes (fishing on the Sabbath, for instance), business licences (for taverns or ferries), and civil disputes, but appointed most community officials, from hog reeve (he rounded up any stray swine that got loose) and fence viewer (he settled neighbours' disputes about fence repairs, etc.) to overseer of the poor. Records from these courts from the early nineteenth century often survive, and by mid-century, local newspapers usually printed lists of the appointments made each year.

- Court of Quarter Session minutes provide an ongoing record of local events; it is surprising what a multitude of community activities they were concerned with until well into the 1840s.

- Where New Englanders settled, they brought with them their tradition of town meetings and town books. The few town books that survive from the eighteenth century not only deal with local administration, they also record family data that shows who belonged in the township.

- Quarter Session records rarely contain full family data, but where marriage was viewed as a civil contract, justices of the peace or town clerks had to register the event in the court minutes.

You can learn more about the legal system of Upper Canada (Ontario) and what records there might be in Janice Nickerson's *Crime and Punishment in Upper Canada: A Researcher's Guide* (Toronto: OGS/Dundurn Press, 2010).

Quebec Civil Law and the Notary

Unlike the rest of Canada, where civil law is based on British Common Law, in Quebec it is based on French law. The Quebec Act of 1774 reinstated French civil law, the seigneurial system of holding land, and the right of the Roman Catholic church to collect the tithe. The actual laws changed over the next century, and today we refer to Quebec as using the Napoleonic Code. While the notary public is part of both our British and French legal heritage, in that province the notary has greater prominence.[4]

Under the unique Quebec Civil Code, notaries do much of the day-to-day work that lawyers perform in other jurisdictions. Since the notary must be literate and educated he, with the parish priest and seigneur, once formed a triumvirate of power and authority in any Quebec community.

Everyone Uses Notaries

In Quebec, everyone uses notaries for drawing up mortgages or deeds of sale, marriage contracts, and wills, as well as for the administration of estates without probate. He was also often the local mortgage broker. Thus, he had a wide grasp of financial affairs in his region, most of which passed through his hands one way or another. The following are the most common notarial records.

- Mortgages and deeds of sale: the village notary was involved in almost every land transfer. Remember, wives had dower rights in the family home, and a married man could not sell the property without his wife's consent. Such documents of consent (et ux) should be with any bill of sale.

- Estates: the Quebec Civil Code provides for holograph wills, wills signed before witnesses, and those drawn up by a notary. In the case of a notarized will, however, the notary is empowered to distribute the estate without formal probate. An estate administered by a notary almost always includes a very detailed inventory of property with value of items. As well, guardianship papers were required for minor children if one parent died, naming a second guardian (*tuteur/tutrice*).

- Marriage contracts: until 1 July 1970, the Quebec Civil Code assumed "community of property" for any marriage where the spouses did not have a marriage contract. Where the wife brought her own property into a marriage, it was customary to have a notary draw up a contract that confirmed the spouses were separate as to property, compensating the wife for her dower rights, and setting out any other family concerns.

- *Donations entre vifs* are contracts found as early as the 1650s, where elderly people, expecting to die, would use such a document to divide their property among their children while still living, with strict provisions set out for their care and support until their deaths. This eliminated need for a will and probate of the estate.

- Other contracts: apprenticeship documents usually list the parents' names.

- *Engagements*: notaries drew up the fur trade companies' labour contracts (*engagement*) with the voyageurs (*engagé*) who paddled and portaged the great trade canoes to the West, and often contain details about when they left, where they left from, if they were to winter over, and their pay.

Minutes and *Greffes*

Quebec notaries had to keep all contracts and documents (*minutes*) indefinitely. The individual notary's original files are termed his *greffe*, and he normally kept a *registre* (a finding aid or index) of families and documents, or if a researcher is unlucky, a daily list of documents created or *répertoire*.

First Catch Your Notary

Even if your Quebec family spoke English and went to a Protestant church or a Jewish synagogue, do not shrug off notarial records as applying only to francophones and Christians. Everyone in Quebec had a family notary, and notarial records exist from the beginnings of the colony.[5] If you have family documents, a lease, marriage contract, or estate papers, one of these should give the notary's name and the date on the document gives a point in time. Then check the annual lists of the *Chambre des Notaires*.

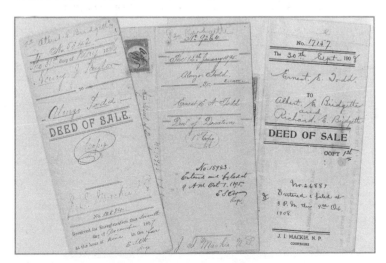

Alonzo Todd's notarial documents. Expect to find a Quebec family using the same notary over many years and several generations.

Chapter 15

Our VIP Heritage

Royal Gazettes

In 1749, when the Board of Trade and Plantations sent an expedition to Nova Scotia to found Halifax, "ships were loaded with everything from fire engines to fishing gear.... There was everything but a printing press."[1] In 1751, Bartholomew Green arrived from Boston with the first printing press; and in March of the following year his partner, John Bushell, printed the maiden issue of the *Halifax Gazette* on that very press.[2] "The *Gazette* was the first newspaper published in what was to become Canada. More than 250 years later it continues to appear every week as the *Royal Gazette*, an official publication of the Nova Scotia government that notifies the public of changes to laws and regulations."[3]

In the British colonies that became Canada, an official government *gazette* was issued regularly, almost as soon as the colony was established. As Lieutenant-Governor John Graves Simcoe mused in 1791, "A printer is indispensably necessary."[4] How else was a colonial government to tell the people what they should know and think? Official *gazettes*, under one title or another, still announce government appointments and print notices of new legislation. The early years, however, were precarious for some printers.

1752 *The Halifax Gazette* (closed 1765)

1754 *Quebec Gazette/La Gazette de Québec*

1765 *Nova Scotia Gazette*

1769 *Nova Scotia Chronicle and Weekly Advertiser* (the first independent newspaper in the colony), which was renamed *Nova Scotia Gazette and the Weekly Chronicle* in 1788, and then renamed again as the *Royal Gazette and Nova Scotia Advertiser*

1778 *La Gazette du commerce et littéraire, pour la ville et district de Montréal* (closed 1779; Canada's first French-language newspaper, edited by Valentin Jutard)

1783 *Royal St. John's* [sic] *Gazette and Nova-Scotia Intelligencer* continued as the *Saint John Gazette and Weekly Advertiser* (non-government)

1785 *The Royal Gazette and New Brunswick Advertiser*

1785 *Montreal Gazette/La Gazette de Montreal* (still publishing)

1793 *The Upper Canada Gazette or American Oracle*

Although most of these papers depended on government subsidies, their early issues were not devoted entirely to government pronouncements. To survive, they needed advertising and readers who would pay for subscriptions.

A typical colonial paper supplemented the official notices with news of ships' movements, as well as a few dozen lines of local news items. The occasional marriage and death notices were limited to very important people, and the best most family historians can hope for is some paid notice about an estate.

The bulk of their content was material lifted from British and American newspapers. Publishers and editors had to tread a fine line. As Chris Raible reminds us: "The editor's employers were British officials ... responsible to the British Crown.... Their interests, their hearts, their homes were essentially English — news to them was British news." The readers, however, "had nearly all come to Upper Canada from the United States.... For them, American events and politics were of more interest, and, undoubtedly exercised more influence."[5]

That dichotomy would apply in other colonies as well as Upper Canada, and while Raible's article recounts the tribulations of several of the early printers, Jobb's concentrated on Bushell's difficulties in Halifax. However, for most social historians, it is the advertisements by local businesses and the lists of official appointments to local positions that are of primary interest.

In most colonies, moreover, publishers of other political persuasions were soon at work, and even a small town might have a number of rival papers.[6] Where this is the case, always check all papers. Your family may have notices only in the one whose politics they favoured.

Almanacs

> **almanac** — n. a register of the days, weeks, and months of the year, with astronomical events, anniversaries, etc.[7]

With those eighteenth and nineteenth century "Almanacks" it will be the "etc." they include that will typically interest family historians.

- Most include lists of civil officials, clergymen, doctors, notaries, and lawyers within the colony, as well as dates of court terms and many local bylaws.

- For match-making mothers, the army officers serving in the province are listed, together with officers of the militia and officers of H.M. Naval Yard, as well as ships of the Royal Navy serving in the region with the names of their officers.

- Travellers may find useful information, such as the days the stagecoaches leave for other places, what ships or ferries operate between local ports, and how long such journeys could take. Tide tables are a staple in Maritime publications since those may influence ship sailings.

- Salaries of Officers of State in England and the United States were given in the *New Brunswick Almanack* for 1843: the first lord of the treasury (the prime minister) received £6,000; the lord high chancellor £14,000. The president of the United States was paid $25,000 per annum. The *Canadian Mercantile Almanack* (Toronto, 1849) tells us that in Canada the governor general received £7,777/15/6, the chief justice of Upper Canada, £1,000/13/4, and the provincial geologist £555/11/0.

Eighteenth and Nineteenth Century Magazines

Researchers should not overlook the early magazines published in Britain, and later in the colonies. They can be a fascinating window into the past. *The Monthly Chronicle* began in 1728, offering a sober chronicle of the month's news and a list of books published, priced at 1 shilling. When, in 1731, the *Gentleman's Magazine* offered news, books, essays, poems, and more for sixpence, it quickly outdistanced the competition. It was around this time that publishers adopted the term "magazine."

- Some of the magazines published in the British Isles had long lives. The *Gentleman's Magazine* existed for 176 years, the *New Monthly Magazine* for 70, while the *Monthly Chronicle* changed its title after four years, but as the *London Magazine* was published for another 53. Most of those published in the colonies were relatively short-lived.

- Their contents ranged from essays, history, archaeology, poetry, and book reviews, to current politics and war news.

- Many British magazines and a few early Canadian periodicals included one or more pages of brief notices of births, marriages, deaths, promotions, and sometimes bankruptcies, or *b-r-p-ts*.

- Announcements were not restricted to the gentry: multiple births, extreme old age, or unusual marriage partners were reported from all walks of life, and the executions were frequently included. None is as replete as the *Gentleman's Magazine*, although those from north of the border are best served by *The Scots Magazine*, while *Walker's Hibernian Magazine* concentrates on the Irish.

SOME EARLY MAGAZINES	
("The" has been omitted in most titles.)	
British Periodicals, available on microfilm, with annual indexes.[8]	
British Magazine	1746–1747
British Magazine or Monthly Repository	1760–1767
European Magazine	1782–1826, merged with

Monthly Magazine	1796–1843
Gentleman's Magazine	1731–1907
Monthly Chronicle	1728–1731, continued as
London Magazine	1732–1785
New Series, 1, 2, 3,	1820–1829
New Monthly Magazine	1814–1884
Scots Magazine	1739–1817, continued as
Edinburgh Magazine	1810–1826
Town and Country Magazine	1767–1796
Universal Magazine	1747–1815
Walker's Hibernian Magazine (Dublin)	1771–1811

Some Periodicals Published in British North America

General

Acadian Magazine, Halifax NS	1826–28
Amarantha, Saint John NB	1841–43
Canadian Magazine and Literary Repository, Montreal	1823–25

There were several short-lived magazines that used the title *Canadian Magazine* in 1833 & 1871–2

Canadian Monthly, Toronto	1872–78
Rose-Bedford's Canadian Monthly, Toronto	1878–82
Week, Toronto	1883–96
Canadian Review and Magazine, Montreal	1824–26
Literary Garland, Montreal	1838–51

Maple Leaf Annual, Toronto	1847, 1848, 1849
Montreal Museum, Montreal	1833–34
Nova Scotia Magazine, Halifax	1789–93
People's Magazine, Montreal	1846–47
Quebec Magazine, Quebec	1792–94
Scribbler, Montreal	1821–27
Snowdrop (for children), Montreal	1847–52
Victoria Magazine, Belleville,ON	1848–49
The Westminster	1896–1916
Denominational	
The Banner (Free Church of Scotland),Toronto	1843–48
British North American Wesleyan Methodist Mag., Saint John	1841–47
Christian Guardian, Toronto	1821–1925
The Wesleyan, Halifax	1838–52

Colonel, Justice of the Peace, or Member of the Legislative Assembly?

"Grandfather Smith was a Major in the Army, we have his commission." Statements like this are not uncommon, and many families treasure such documents in the fond belief that their ancestor served with the British Army. If they happened to actually read the commission, though, they will likely learn that he was really an officer of the county militia, a volunteer military force raised from the civil population, assisting the regular army in emergencies.

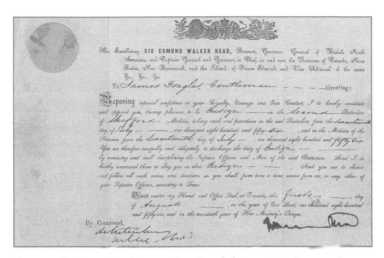

Six years after James Douglas arrived in Canada East in 1850, he received a commission as an Ensign in the Shefford Militia. His Excellency, Sir Edmund Walker Head, Baronet, was governor general of British North America at the time.

- Under the Lower Canada Militia Act of 1803 and the Upper Canada Militia Act of 1808, the militia was composed of all able-bodied men (except Quakers and others whose religious convictions forbade military service) between the ages of 16 and 60. Attendance at the annual muster of the militia was compulsory. Training might depend on what regular army officers (active service or half-pay) were available in the area.

- As the threats of American invasion lessened, the militia became more of a community social activity, and the annual muster often turned into a general carouse as His or Her Majesty's health was pledged over and over again.

- Each county had one or more regiments of militia with a colonel, lieutenant-colonel, major, eight to a dozen captains, and equivalent numbers of lieutenants and ensigns. A lot of civilians held commissions, and many of these impressive signed and sealed documents survive as family treasures.

- Family tradition often gets the details wrong, but such commissions can indicate that a particular ancestor was a man of some standing in the community. The colonel of the militia regiment was an important person locally, if not provincially.

Tradition also tends to exaggerate political careers by claiming that an ancestor was an important member of parliament (M.P.P.) or member of the legislative assembly(M.L.A.), while research may show he was actually a long-serving justice of the peace (J.P.) who won a single election and served one brief term in a short-lived government. To verify legends about these V.I.P. ancestors, consult local almanacs that were published annually in many colonies. As well, there are published lists of members of provincial legislatures of the colonies and provinces, though some may cover pre-1841, 1841–1867, and post-Confederation in separate volumes.

British Titles and Honours

Ten Ladies dancing,
Eleven Lords a leaping ...
And a Peer in the Family Tree?

Many Victorian family historians hoped to find "noble blood" when they took up the hunt for their ancestors. In North America, then as now, very few people understood much about titles, honours, or their proper usage, but they delighted in them nonetheless. Having the same family name as a "Lord" or "Sir" almost always leads to tales of noble descent. Unsubstantiated myths abound, but a grain of truth sometimes lurks in family tradition.

- Peers of the British Isles, their families, and most collateral lines are well-documented from the eighteenth century on. The lineages of most of the noble families of Europe are also readily available in print. Knights and baronets are all on record, though their families are not quite as easy to track down. For them you can check the *Gentleman's Magazine*.

- Over the past three centuries, a great many young, unmarried, male members of noble families served in North America with the British Army and Navy, or as assistants to the various peers and royals who came to fill positions of authority. However, while the legitimate progeny of titled families are very easy to verify, their "natural children" are not, since they would not be listed in peerages.

At one time in Canada, British honours were standard issue for politicians and people of wealth. Almost every prime minister received a knighthood or baronetcy: Sir Wilfred Laurier (G.C.M.G.), Sir John A. MacDonald (G.C.B.), Sir Charles Tupper (Bart.), to name just three. Also, more than one wealthy financier or industrialist was made a baronet, so we have Sir James Dunn (Bart.) or Sir Harry Oakes (Bart.). Military leaders, like Sir Arthur Currie, were often appointed to one of the orders of knighthood (Garter, Bath, St. Michael, or St. George), while medical men, lawyers, and educators were more likely to become the less prestigious knight bachelor (K.B.), i.e. one not belonging to a special order.

- Baronets and knights are neither peers nor lords, a fact that escapes most North American news editors. Both titles are honours: baronetcies can be inherited, knighthoods cannot.

- A woman cannot be knighted, but may be honoured with D.B.E. (Dame of the Most Excellent Order of the British Empire), which is styled as "Dame."

- Men with either honour are called "Sir," and to distinguish between them when writing, a baronet may have Bt. or Bart. after his name. Their wives are styled "Lady *Husband's Surname*," since most married women have historically taken their style of address from their husbands.

- The main historical exceptions are women who held titles in their own right. A woman can, under some circumstances, inherit a barony, and the daughters of certain peers are styled as "Lady *First Name*" (see below).

- Biographical entries for any Sir Canadian Politician will give the date they were knighted, or made K.G., K.C.B., G.C.M.G., etc. Most dictionaries or biographical dictionaries list the letters-after-the-name that these honours generate under Abbreviations. Wives are styled "Lady *Husband's Surname.*"

And a Peer in the Maple Tree?

Since the Parliament of Canada adopted the Nickel Resolution in 1919, no Canadian government has recommended citizens for British honours bearing titles. However, Canadian newspaper publishers do like being called "Press Lords," and many have accepted peerages, but such barons as Lord Beaverbrook (Max Aitken) and Lord Thomson of Fleet (Roy Thomson) left Canada and gained their honours in England, as did Prime Minister R.B. Bennett, who was created Viscount Bennett of Mickleham on 16 July 1941. Lord Black of Crossharbour is also well known.

"Yes m'lord. No m'lady."

There is an exact protocol for the titles used when addressing or referring to the nobility that will tell you a lot if the titles are properly used. Alas, in North America they rarely are.

- "Lord" and "Lady" are *not* titles. They are styles of address, like Mr., Mrs., or Dr. Not all men who are called Lord are peers, nor do all sit in the House of Lords.

• In Great Britain, there are five ranks in the peerage. In ascending order, they are: baron, viscount, earl, marquess (often seen in the French spelling *marquis*), and duke. Their wives are respectively: baroness, viscountess, countess, marchioness, and duchess. Except for dukes and duchesses, they are all addressed as Lord or Lady. In England only the actual holder of the peerage sat in the House of Lords.

• By courtesy, the eldest sons of dukes, marquesses, and earls take their father's secondary titles. If the heir to the title has a son, he in turn bears a lesser or junior title.

• Younger sons of dukes and marquesses also prefix the style Lord to their first and surnames (e.g. Lord Peter Whimscy), and their wives are styled as Lady, but the husband's first name should always be used in such courtesy titles (e.g. Lady Peter Whimsey). Such Lords may be elected to the House of Commons.

• Daughters of dukes, marquesses, and earls are also entitled to use the prefix Lady with their first name. For example, Lady Diana Spencer was the daughter of Earl Spencer (not the Earl *of* Spencer: please note that this is one of a few titles that does not include an "of").

- Younger sons of earls are called "the Honourable," as are all children of viscounts and barons.

- When a Lady Jane or Lady Mary Moorhen turns up in family tradition, you would be wise to suspect a title is being misused. If you actually do have the daughter of a duke, marquess, or earl in your pedigree, it is easily verified in older Peerages or Extinct Peerages, but be sure to check the Irish Peerages as well.

Here we must note that there is also the Peerage of Scotland, as well as one of Ireland, with the same ranks and the same forms of address, but with different political and social standing. This can be confusing, since a man can be a peer of Scotland (fourth Earl of Rosebery, for example) and a peer of the United Kingdom (first Baron Rosebery) at the same time.

Lordships for Sale

One curious title that occasionally turns up, usually with some headline like "Peer sells 900 year old Title!", is Lord (and Lady) of the Manor. In Britain, for 500 years after the Norman conquest, the manor (an agricultural estate) was the unit of local government. Its head was the Lord of the Manor (literally a landlord, not necessarily a titled person) who held the land from the king and governed through the Manor Court. The power to create new manors ended with the thirteenth century, and over the ensuing centuries many of these titles have disappeared. Those that remain usually date back to the Middle Ages, and the title goes with the land.

Today, if you buy such a manor, you become the Lord of that Manor, and you and your wife may call yourselves James and Mary Smith, Lord and Lady of the Manor of Wherever. Shortened to "Lord and Lady of Wherever," it impresses North American tourists no end.

French and European Titles

- French titles are complicated, because there are pre-revolutionary titles (which are the oldest and, some think, best) and those granted by Napoleon to reward his friends and supporters (denigrated by royalists). And finally, there were titles granted by the restored King Louis XVIII (he was broke and titles were cheap) and subsequent rulers. They are quite well-sorted by Albert Reverend, in a series of variously titled volumes, that were kept up to date for many years in his *Annuaire de la Noblesse*.

- In Europe, there are papal titles, as well as those granted by various monarchs and emperors. Some were inherited by the eldest child, some by all children, resulting in a plethora of princes and princesses. Take care and double check with someone who understands the systems in use in the specific country. Remember that dates matter.

- The constantly shifting borders of European countries make things even more compli-cated, but the *Almanac de Gotha, 1763–1944,* is the standard pre–Second World War refer-ence work, while a new multi-volume series, *Genealogisches Handbuch des Adels, 1951–,* is slowly working its way through the entire nobility of Europe.

Chapter 16

Our Seafaring and Military Heritage

Dockyards and Garrisons

In the seventeenth and eighteenth centuries, "the Lion and the Unicorn were fighting for the crown" across much of the world. Both the British and the French navies had keen eyes for a good harbour, particularly where a height of land allowed the army engineers to build a fort for defence. Thus we have Quebec City, which was colonized at the beginning of the seventeenth century, and Halifax founded in 1749 — both of which reflect these requirements. Many other cities have also benefited from having an army garrison or naval base.

- British regiments served in Canada until the Treaty of Washington in 1871.[1] Aside from their actual military duties, British regiments made a lasting contribution to the colonies by their services as surveyors, engineers, and builders of roads and canals. The Royal Navy not only defended our coasts and shipping, they saw that our waters and harbours were charted by able men, such as Captain James Cook.[2]

- A regiment or naval station also enriched the social and cultural life of the garrison towns and cities: their bands often played concerts, the officers might put on theatrical entertainments, or throw balls. Some soldiers married (some did not), and their children might be born in several ports or towns as the posting of a man's regiment or ship changed.

By the last quarter of the nineteenth century, the British navy was using steam power. Here we see two of the older three-masted ships-of-the-line beside a modern steam-powered vessel, as well as a sailor-powered longboat and a couple of tiny sailboats.

Halifax Was Both

Within 10 years of its founding, the "Halifax Dockyard began to take its new important shape."[3] Halifax became the northern hub for the Royal Navy's North Atlantic station (Bermuda was the other) and "facilities at the Halifax Naval Yard were first rate." Charles Austen (Jane's brother) relied on them for repairs to his 20-gun sloop-of-war, the *Indian*, "until after 1809 when comparable services were becoming available at Bermuda." Even so, during the Napoleonic wars, the town was "very much in a naval backwater [as] the war at sea [was] being determined elsewhere."[4] One of the most interesting phenomena taking place in Halifax over a hundred years "was the number of daughters of the well-to-do who married naval husbands and followed them across the seas."[5]

The British Army and the Royal Navy continued to maintain the defence of Canada until 1871, when they withdrew from all but two bases: the Royal Navy's dockyard and small army garrison at Halifax and a naval base at Esquimalt on the Pacific. These bases were handed over to the Canadian Department of Militia and Defence at the beginning of 1906, having been extensively renovated, fully equipped, and left ready for use. The sad decline that followed is another story.[6]

Registers of Shipping and Seamen

In 1878, Canada had the fifth largest merchant fleet in the world. Between 1787 and 1900, 26,803 vessels were built in the three Maritime provinces alone,[7] more along the St. Lawrence and the Great Lakes, and doubtless more still in Pacific shipyards. You should assume that if your ancestors lived near any navigable water they may well have owned a small vessel, or shares in one.

- Vessels were owned in 64 shares, the same number for a 100-ton coastal schooner or the 1,600-ton ship *Marco Polo*. This means that, in theory, there could be 64 owners. I have found vessels with up to 24 owners, but a more typical number is four to six business associates or family members.

- Since 1786, British laws required registration for vessels over 15 tons burthen, owned by any of His or Her Majesty's subjects (see Chapter 14). In 1824, the registration form was altered to show not only the type and size of the vessel but also each owner's full name, place of residence, and occupation. The registers of ships built in Canada are available on microfilm from Library and Archives Canada.

Here's some tall-ships vocabulary; for fuller details see Charles Armour's *Sailing Ships of the Maritimes* and W.E.F. Ward's *The Royal Navy and the Slavers*:[8]

Square-rigged: square sails set on horizontal spars called yards, roughly at right angles to the long axis of the vessel.

Fore-and-aft: the familiar sailboat and schooner rig. Canadians can see an example of it, the famous *Bluenose*, on the 10¢ coin.

Ship: a large sailing vessel, square-rigged on three (or more) masts.

Barque: a vessel with three or more masts, the aftermost mast (mizzenmast) fore-and-aft rigged, the others square rigged.

Barquentine: a vessel with three or more masts, square-rigged only on the foremast, all others fore-and-aft.

Brig: a two-masted vessel, both square-rigged.

Brigantine: a two-masted vessel, foremast square rigged, mainmast for-and-aft.

Schooner: a vessel with two or more masts, all fore-and-aft rigged.

Tern schooner: three-masted schooner.

Topsail schooner: has one or two square-rigged topsails on her foremast.

Family members may have also been sailors, mates, or masters of vessels. For Great Britain and British colonies, the Board of Trade kept detailed records of both the ships and those who sailed in them.

Master: the officer in command of a merchant vessel (Captain), must hold a Master's Certificate of Competency. These are well-documented.

Mate: second-in-command of a merchant vessel, must have a Mate's Certificate of Competency, also well-documented.

In 1995, *Families*, the Ontario Genealogical Society journal, published Roberta Thomas's article, "The Maritime History Archive, Memorial University of Newfoundland: Sources for Research," explaining how Britain's Public Record Office transferred most of the records of the Registrar General of Shipping and Seamen, the bulk of which comprised the Agreements and Accounts of Crew of British Empire vessels, 1863–1912, 1913–1938, and 1951–1976, to Memorial University.

Her article details the complex division that left a portion of the records in Great Britain, and describes the extensive related holdings of the Maritime History Archive. It also notes the work done by the Atlantic Shipping Project between 1976 and 1982.[9]

Atlantic Shipping Database

This project set out to produce a computerized database of ship registrations. In the 1970s, computer memories were small and every byte counted. They limited their base to 10 ports in Atlantic Canada and a sample of the Agreements and Account of Crew from ships registered at four of these ports.

> **Warning to Users**: These databases are *not complete*, however they are available at LAC, on the Internet, and on the CD-ROM, *Ships and Seafarers of Atlantic Canada*.

The database of ships for 1787–1936 was compiled from the Certificates of Registry from 10 ports: three in New Brunswick, five in Nova Scotia, Charlottetown,

Prince Edward Island, and St. John's, Newfoundland. That means this database doesn't include the enormous number of vessels built in other ports some of which later became ports of registry. The project makes this clear whenever and wherever they have the chance. However, people who do not read the fine print may assume that if they can't find a vessel in the database, it wasn't registered in Canada.

> **An Example**: The database includes 17 small vessels built by Robert Andrew Chapman at Rockland, New Brunswick, including those that he registered at Saint John early in his career. It does not include the 14 registered at Dorchester, New Brunswick, after the shiretown became a port of registry.

> **An Example**: St. Martins, New Brunswick, never became a port of registry, but was home to two large fleets belonging to the Vaughan and Moran families. Esther Clarke Wright points out that St. Martins ships were regis-tered not only in Saint John and Halifax, but also further afield in several Irish ports, as well as in Scotland, and Liverpool.[10]

The Atlantic Shipping Project database also contains information on some 20,000 masters and 182,000 seamen and their voyages from Atlantic Canada. This is *a sampling only* from four of those 10 ports. If your ancestor is in it, great, but do not assume that it includes all the voyages he signed on for.

Signals and Communication

When fighting a war it can be very useful to be able to send messages quickly between distant outposts (or ships) and headquarters. Over the centuries, signallers have devised many ways to do this and the ancient systems were quite complex. Most involved flags, shields, or lanterns run up a ship's mast or pole on a tower at the top of a hill.

Admiral Sir Home Riggs Popham devised the very sophisticated system of flag signals that the admiralty adopted for the British Navy in 1803. As early as 1793, however, the French had invented a semaphore telegraph with which Paris could communicate quickly with armies on the borders:

> **Semaphore**: a system of sending messages by holding the arms or two flags in certain positions according to an alphabetic code. And a signalling apparatus consisting of a post with moveable arm or arms, lantern, etc. for use (especially on railways) day and night.[11]

The British countered with a Swedish system to link Whitehall and the Channel Ports. In Nova Scotia, the Duke of Kent devised a system of visual telegraphy using flags and large wickerwork balls and drums by day, and lanterns by night.[12] As you can imagine, these highly visible signal systems were often discussed by the local population.

- Do not be surprised to find the term *telegraph* used long before Samuel Morse demonstrated the electric telegraph in the United States in 1837; Sir Charles Wheatstone (1802–1875) and Sir William Cooke secured a British patent the same year.

- The code Morse devised, an alphabet in which the letters are represented by various combinations of short and long sounds or flashes of light, truly changed communication. It could be used on a telegraph line, and 60 years later, on the wireless telegraph Marconi invented.

- Guglielmo Marconi was granted "the world's first radio patent"[13] in July 1897, based on earlier work by Nikola Tesla and Sir Oliver Lodge.[14] Because the telegraph and telephone already provided overland communication, Marconi directed his invention to shipping, and the Wireless Telegraph and Signal Co. Ltd. was launched.

- Within a few years, Marconi's company was operating a small number of coastal stations in Britain and had equipped a few commercial vessels with his invention. The Canadian Marconi Wireless Telegraphy Company came into being in 1902–03.[15]

- By 1905, ship-to-shore radio had become indispensable in communicating with ocean-going vessels. The demand for the service was so great that new shore stations were constructed on both sides of the Atlantic. "With rare exceptions all the Marconi stations along the Canadian Atlantic coast were on remote capes and islands."[16]

- The operators who ran the shore stations and radio service on commercial vessels were almost all employees of the Marconi Company, and Morse Code was their second language. If your family tree includes a "brass-pounder" or "sparks" working for Marconi in the first quarter of the twentieth century, search out the Canadian author, Thomas H. Raddall (1903–94). In his teens and early twenties, he worked on ships and at the Sable Island station, recounting his experiences in a memoir, several short stories, and the novel *The Nymph and The Lamp* (1950).

British Naval Tradition

Considering Canada's seafaring tradition, we have a very limited naval history because we relied on the Royal Navy's North American Squadron until 1906 when the British departed. Before that, and for some time later, if you wanted a Naval career, you joined the Royal Navy.

- Until the end of the Napoleonic Wars, any Maritimer wanting to fight at sea probably signed on as a privateer, a form of legalized piracy that *Bluenose* merchants were partial to in wartime.

- If you go to *www.bbc.co.uk/history/british/ empire_seapower*, you can read Andrew Lambert's "Life at Sea in the Royal Navy of the 18th Century." It will set you straight on a lot of popular mythinformation.

Many books are available on the history and the records of the Royal Navy. These lists will to help you separate the flag officers from the warrant officers, and a first-rate ship-of-the-line from a sloop-of-war.

Some Pre-1900 Definitions

Ship: a large sailing vessel, square-rigged on three (or more) masts.

Rate: until mid-nineteenth century, a warship was rated by the number of guns she carried.

Ship-of-the-Line: a warship large enough to fight in the line of battle, carrying at least 60 guns.

first-rate: 100 guns or more, three decks of guns, 800 men or more.

second-rate: 75 to 100, three decks of guns.

third-rate: 60 to 74 guns, two decks of guns.

Frigate: smaller ship, built for speed, "the eyes of the fleet."

fourth-rate: 50 guns with some 350 men.

fifth-rate: 25 to 40 guns.

sixth-rate: 24 guns on one deck, some 175 men.

Sloop-of-war: small ship, shallower draft than a warship, 16 to 20 guns.

The Navy also used the small merchant-type vessels described earlier. Most common was a two-masted, square-rigged brig, usually commanded by a lieutenant or commander. The larger naval brigs might be rated as a "Sloop-of-war."

In the Royal Navy, a "Squadron" refers to a portion of the fleet. Nelson's fleet was divided into three squadrons, the senior Red (centre), White (van), and junior Blue (rear), each with their admiral, real admiral, and vice admiral. This scheme remained basically unchanged until 1864.

Some squadron divisions were geographic, e.g. the West Atlantic Squadron.

Commissioned Officers

All HM ships have been commanded by commissioned officers with limited exceptions among small and non-combatant vessels. Unlike the eighteenth and nineteenth century army, commissions were not bought or sold. Naval officers were expected to know something about their job, and most started as midshipmen, working their way up.

For an excellent description of all the subtle distinctions in rank, and changes over time, see N.A.M. Rodger's *Naval Records for Genealogists*.[17]

The British Admiralty had both experienced sailors and politically appointed civilians in its top echelons. The Board of Admiralty was a committee of the Ministry of Defence superintending the Royal Navy.

The senior naval officer serving on the board was called the "First Sea Lord," while other naval members of the board were called "Sea Lords."

Those in command of the fleet were "Flag Officers." These officers were entitled to fly a flag from their flag-ship, and they were:

Lord High Admiral: Admiral of the fleet.

Admiral: commander of a fleet or squadron.

Vice Admiral: a naval officer ranking below an admiral.

Rear Admiral: a naval officer ranking below a vice admiral.

Commodore: a "Post-Captain" temporarily in command of a squadron or other division of a fleet, ordered to hoist a broad pendant.

After 1747, we encounter "Yellow Admirals," who are rear admirals without the distinction of squadron, but with a pension equivalent to that of a rear admiral. This effectively allowed the navy to retire elderly captains and reach down the captain's list for men suited for active flag rank.

Other Commissioned Officers:

Captain or Post Captain: being "Made Post" is to be appointed to command a sixth-rate ship or better. Once a man achieves this rank promotion was automatic by seniority for those in active service.

Commander: a naval officer next in rank below a captain.

Lieutenant-Commander: lieutenant in command of a non-post vessel.

Lieutenant: a naval officer next in rank below a lieutenant-commander.

Sub-Lieutenant: a naval officer ranking next below a lieutenant.

Midshipman: is a naval officer of rank between a naval cadet and a sub-lieutenant.

Warrant Officers: The list includes master, surgeon (and mates), purser, boatswain, gunner, carpenter, cook, chaplain, armourer, schoolmaster, and sailmaker. Engineers and sparks come along later.

N.A.M. Rodger calls the warrant officers "a disparate group."[18] Warrant sea officers were the heads of specialized technical branches of the ship's company for which they were responsible to the captain directly. Their role changed as naval technology changed. Rodger sorts through them, detailing how things changed over time with charts and clear explanations.

Master is the term used for the commanding officer or captain of a merchant vessel, but in the Royal Navy he is the "Warrant Officer of Commissioned Rank." When James Cook passed the examinations for his master's warrant and was appointed sailing master of HMS *Pembroke* (60 guns) he was expected to be proficient in navigation, but his job also "entailed taking soundings and bearings and observing the appearance of coasts. Masters were expected to add to and correct existing charts."[19]

According to Admiralty regulations a sailing master was also required to inspect all provisions and stores sent on board, to see that ballast was adequate and properly stowed, to ensure that the rigging and sails were in working order, and that the compasses, hour glasses, log and lead lines were preserved in good order.[20]

> **Ratings**: ranking beneath the officers of all sorts are the ordinary sailors rated by their captain to a position that was both rank and job. Note: *Rating* refers to a non-commissioned sailor, and has nothing to do with the rates of ships.

The Royal Canadian Navy (1910–1968)

When the Royal Navy left Halifax in 1906, Canada was given a totally renovated and operational dockyard and garrison, but in Ottawa, and far from the sea, the government had no navy and little interest in building one. Despite their reluctance, the Naval Service of Canada is now a hundred years old.[21] Ottawa tentatively established it in 1910 when the cruiser *Niobe* (second-hand from the Royal Navy) was berthed at the Halifax Dockyard where she "remained alone and forlorn at Halifax, saving on bunker bills, slowly going aground on her own beer bottles."[22]

Canada's naval contribution to the First World War was minimal, having one decrepit cruiser on each coast and, in Halifax, a "collection of armed steamers, converted yachts, drifters, trawlers and motor-boats" whose purpose was to patrol the coast and keep the approaches to Halifax harbour swept for mines every day. Many Canadians served in the Royal Navy, and "Halifax became, as in the old wars, a Royal Navy base."[23]

The Wavy Navy

I was a small child in the 1930s, and can remember when we had two-thirds of the Royal Canadian Navy at anchor in Shediac Bay. The third ship was on the west coast. The number of ships in our navy may have been a source of jokes, but the men who served on those ships weren't, nor are they today.

- The Royal Canadian Navy had three components: the RCN was the regular, professional navy; the RCNR (Royal Canadian Naval Reserve) was composed of merchant seamen and men with sea experience; and the RCNVR (Royal Canadian Naval Volunteer Reserve) was for landsmen. When the Second World War started and men enlisted for "the duration," they joined the RCNVR.

- To distinguish them from regular officers who wore straight gold rank stripes on their jacket cuffs, RCNVR officers wore undulating or wavy stripes, and ratings wore similar stripes on their large uniform collars. That's how it came to be that our "Wavy Navy" manned the corvettes, escorted convoys, and patrolled the north Atlantic.[24]

- There are several books about Canada's war in the North Atlantic, among them James B. Lamb's *Corvette Navy*, Mac Johnston's *Corvettes Canada*, and Marc Milner's *North Atlantic Run*.

- Ashore in Halifax, Ottawa-style attitudes prevailed: "the enormous shore bureaucracy seemed most concerned with its own well being, and considered the ships a contemptuous nuisance, interfering with the orderly administration of its internal operations. Everything closed down after five and on week-ends."[25]

Canadian armed forces were unified by the Trudeau government in 1968, and all the services changed to green uniforms. The traditional uniforms were restored in 1985, but not the Royal Canadian Navy or Royal Canadian Air Force. Today we refer to the Naval Service of Canada. Our sailors are as professional and as brave as they always were, but they are no longer royal.

Ottawa in 1882–84. The Post Office. Horses and carriages are crossing "Sappers' Bridge, a solid stone structure built by the military" as part of the Rideau Canal. Sappers were the royal Engineers. To the right is the Dufferin Bridge, "a new, well-designed viaduct of iron." Lord Dufferin was the Governor General at the time.

British Military Tradition

If you ever served in the armed forces, you know how the top brass are ranked and the difference between a sergeant major and a staff sergeant. If you don't know, there is a place to find the answers on the Internet: the *Canadian Military History Gateway*, with an excellent glossary that explains the difference between a field marshal and a brigadier, as well as a corps, battalion, and squadron.

The Canadian Military follows many traditions of the British Army, one being the practice of calling both private soldiers and some officers by different terms according to what branch of the service they are with. This brief glossary explains a few of these terms and some used in earlier times.

> **Subaltern**: junior commissioned officer assisting a captain.
>
> **Ensign**: now called a second lieutenant, it's the lowest rank of commissioned officer in the infantry.
>
> **Coronet**: the lowest rank of commissioned officer in the cavalry.
>
> **Bombardier**: corporal in the artillery.
>
> **Private**: an infantryman or soldier in a general administrative unit. *Private* originally meant a private citizen who hired himself out for service in the army. The following rank as privates:
>
>> **Aircraftman**: the lowest rank in the air force

Gunner: serves with the artillery

Rifleman: serves in a rifle regiment

Sapper: the engineers who built forts, bridges, canals, railways

Signaller: serves in the signal corps

Sniper: an expert marksman [sharp shooter] armed with a rifle

Trooper: originally cavalry, now with the armoured corps

As you research the armies of the past, you will encounter many other terms that define what certain other soldiers did.

Dragoon: originally a cavalryman who dismounted and fought with early types of pistols that sent out a flame like a dragon. By the time of Napoleon, they were simply cavalry soldiers.

Fencible: a soldier enlisted for defensive service in his own country.

Fusilier: a member of any regiment formerly armed with fusils. A fusil was a light musket.

Grenadier: originally, taller and stronger men who could throw grenades.

Hussar: a light cavalryman, originally in the Hungarian army, noted for elaborate uniforms.

Lancers: light cavalry armed with lances, originally Polish.

Musketeer: a soldier armed with a musket, a light gun used by infantrymen.

Some other terms you may encounter:

Brevet: a brevet commission entitles the holder to be called by the next rank higher than the one he holds. A brevet-major would be a captain acting as a major, but without the higher pay of the higher rank.

Guards: the army units who protected the sovereign. In Britain the units were the Life Guards and Royal Horse Guards (both cavalry), the Foot Guards (infantry), the Grenadier, Scots, and Coldstream Guards.

Half-Pay: a payment to both army and naval officers to keep them on the active list and ready to be called back into service, but often a preliminary step to retirement. In Canada, British half-pay officers given land grants were expected to train and support the local militia.

Ordnance: mounted guns or cannons; hence a branch of the military dealing with ammunition and military stores and materials.

Ordnance Survey: in the U.K. an official survey organization, originally under the master of the ordnance, that prepares large scale detailed maps.

Provost: army police force, military police.

Town Major: the chief executive officer (staff officer) in a garrison town or fortress; sometimes an officer who had married and remained behind on half-pay when his regiment left the colony.

Gunner C.S. Douglas served in the artillery in the First World War. Gunner Douglas and friends at Petawawa had this photograph printed on postcard stock to send to their friends.

Appendix

Some Useful Historical Dates

1598	Edict of Nantes, gives French Protestants religious freedom
1601	British East India Company's first voyage
1603	Champlain's first voyage to New France
	24 March, Queen Elizabeth I dies, James I ascends to the throne
1604	October, De Mont's expedition winters on Île Ste-Croix
1605	Port Royal founded, first Acadian settlement
1606	British ships fly Jack of Andrew & George crosses
1607	English establish colony at Jamestown, Virginia
1608	Champlain founds French settlement at Quebec

1609	Independence of seven United Dutch Provinces established
1610	Scots and English settle in Ulster
	Tea introduced to Europe
1611	Authorized version of *The Holy Bible* published
1618	Start of Thirty Years War (1618–1648)
1620	Pilgrims arrive at Plymouth Rock in the *Mayflower*
1624	James I declares war on Spain
1625	27 March, James I dies, Charles I ascends to the throne
1626	Manhattan bought by Dutch and named New Amsterdam
1630	Treaty of Madrid ends war with Spain
1633	English trading posts established in Bengal
1642	22 August, Outbreak of Civil War in England
1643	Accession of Louis XIV of France
1648	24 October, Thirty Year War ends with Peace of Westphalia
1649	30 January, execution of Charles I
	19 May, England declared a Commonwealth
1651	3 September, Battle of Worcester: defeated by Cromwell, Prince Charles flees to France;
	First Navigation Act
1652	Africa, Cape Colony established by Dutch
1653	Oliver Cromwell becomes Lord Protector

1658   3 September, Oliver Cromwell dies, Richard Cromwell made Lord Protector

1659   25 May, Richard Cromwell resigns

1660   29 May, Charles II (–1685) enters London, the monarchy is restored

1662   May, Act of Uniformity restores Anglican Church

1663   Edict, signed by Louis XIV, creating the Sovereign Council of Quebec to govern the royal province of New France

1664   British annex New Netherlands, Manhattan renamed New York

1666   2–6 September, Great Fire of London, rats killed, plague ends

1670   Hudson's Bay Company granted Charter and control of Rupert's Land

1673   March, Test Act excludes Roman Catholics from public office

1683   Seige of Vienna by the Turks

1685   6 February, Charles II dies, James II ascends throne

Revocation of the Edict of Nantes (1598) by Louis XIV

1688   5 November, The "Glorious Revolution," William of Orange lands at Torbay, enters London 19 December; James II, wife, and son flee to France

1689   February, William III (died 8 March 1702) & Mary II (died 28 December 1694) proclaimed King and Queen

1690	12 July, Battle of the Boyne, William II defeats James II
1692	13 February, Glencoe, massacre of Macdonalds by Campbells
	Salem witch trials begin
1695	Naval Dockyard established at Plymouth
1697	Treaty of Ryswick between England, France, Holland, and Spain ends Nine Years War
1701	War of the Spanish Succession (–1713)
1702	8 March, death of William III, Queen Anne ascends throne (–1714)
1704	Capture of Gibraltar by Sir George Rooke
1707	12 May, union of England and Scotland; Scottish Parliament abolished; Union Jack with crosses of St. Andrew and St. George
1710	13 October, British capture Port Royal and rename it Annapolis Royal
1713	11 April, Treaty of Utrecht; British title to Newfoundland and mainland Nova Scotia established; France retains Île-Royale, Île St-Jean and lands north of Chignecto
1714	1 August, death of Queen Anne, George I ascends throne (–1727)
1715	1 September, death of Louis XIV, Louis XV infant, regency of Duc d'Orleans
1725	8 February, death of Peter the Great of Russia
1727	11 June, death of George I, George II ascends throne (–1760)

1740	Holy Roman Empire; 20 October, death of Charles VI, Marie Theresa (1717–1780)
	War of the Austrian Succession (–1748)
	Accession of Frederick II ("Frederick the Great") of Prussia
1745	17 June, Louisbourg surrendered to British
	23 July, Charles Edward Stuart lands in Scotland
1746	16 April, Battle of Culloden, Charles Edward Stuart flees to France
1748	18 October, Treaty of Aix-la-Chapelle, Louisbourg returned to France
1749	9 July, Halifax founded
1752	14 September, Britain adopts Gregorian Calendar
1753	Act for the naturalization of Jews in England
1755	June, British capture French forts in Chignecto, begin expulsion of Acadians from Nova Scotia
	November, Lisbon earthquake
1756	Seven Years War begins (–1763)
	Black Hole of Calcutta
1758	26 July, British recapture Louisbourg
1759	13 September, Battle of the Plains of Abraham at Quebec City
1760	8 September, Capitulation of Montreal: Canada surrendered to British
	25 October, death of George II, accession of George III (–1820)

1762 17 July, accession of Catherine the Great of Russia

France hands over Louisiana Territory to Spain

1763 10 February, Treaty of Paris ends Seven Years War. France cedes Canada and remaining colonies in Acadia to Great Britain

7 October, Royal Proclamation of 1763: establishes boundaries and governments for new colonies, Canada renamed Province of Quebec

1764 16 July, Acadians allowed to return to Nova Scotia

10 August, Establishment of civil government in Province of Quebec

1767 American colonies impose taxes on tea, paper, and other goods

1770 April, Captain Cook sails into Botany Bay, Australia

1773 16 December, Boston Tea Party

1774 May 10, Louis XVI becomes king of France

5 September, First Continental Congress meets at Philadelphia

Quebec Act, authorized French Civil Law and Roman Catholic religion

1775 September, American Army invades Canada, takes Montreal, attacks Quebec

1776 1 July, American Declaration of Independence

1778 29 March, Captain James Cook sights land at Vancouver Island

1780   June, Gordon Riots in London

Death of Maria Theresa of Austria, succession of Joseph II

1783   3 September, Treaty of Paris (Treaty of Separation) establishes United States of America, exodus of Loyalists to British North America

1784   November, New Brunswick and Cape Breton become separate colonies

Methodists split from Church of England

1787   17 September, signing of American constitution

1788   U.K. Parliamentary motion for abolition of the Slave trade

First convicts sent to Australia

1789   14 July, Paris, storming of the Bastille

1791   20 June, Louis XVI attempting to flee, turned back at Varennes

26 December, Canada or Constitutional Act (passed 10 June) in force; Province of Quebec split into Lower Canada and Upper Canada

1792   Captain George Vancouver enters Burrard Inlet

1792   13 August, French royal family imprisoned

1793   Upper Canada prohibits importation of slaves, legislates first marriage act

21 January, execution of Louis XVI of France

1 February, France declares war on Britain and Holland

First coalition formed against France by Britain, Austria, Prussia, Holland, and Spain

1794	19 November, Jay's Treaty signed between United States and Britain
1795	November, Rule of the Directory in France
1796	Spring, Bonaparte invades Italy, enters Milan
1798	1 August, Battle of the Nile. Nelson destroys French fleet
1799	Napoleon Bonaparte overthrows Directory, becomes First Consul
1800	Louisiana Territory returned to France
1801	1 January, Union of Great Britain and Ireland to form United Kingdom
	Union Jack (place Patrick over Andrew, George on top)
1802	27 March, Peace of Amiens between Britain and France
1803	April, U.S. purchases Louisiana from France
	18 May, Britain and France at war again
1805	Battle of Trafalgar; 21 October, death of Nelson
	2 December, Battle of Austerlitz, Napoleon defeats Austrians and Russians
1807	March, Slave trade prohibited in all British possessions
1808	August, Peninsula War; British expeditionary force lands in Spain
	30 August, French forces withdraw from Portugal
1809	16 January, Battle of Corunna; Sir John Moore fatally wounded

April, British forces under Arthur Wellesley land in Portugal

18 July, Wellesley defeats French at Talavera,

4 September, Wellesley created Viscount Wellington of Talavera, so will now be referred to as "Wellington" rather than "Wellesley"

1810   February, Napoleon marries Marie-Louise of Austria

1811   Insanity of George III, Prince of Wales becomes Regent

March, England, Luddites start destroying factory machinery

1812   June, U.S. declares war, invades Upper Canada; War of 1812

The Earl of Selkirk's Scottish settlers arrive at the junction of the Red and Assiniboine Rivers

22 July, Wellington defeats French at Salamanca

12 August, Wellington enters Madrid, created Marquess 18 August

14 September, Napoleon enters Moscow; a month later French begin retreat

1813   October, Wellington enters France

Battle of Leipzig, Napoleon defeated, Prussian army enters France

1814   30–31 March, Allies enter Paris, Napoleon abdicates, exiled to Elba

18 April, Armistice signed, Peninsular War ends

3 May, Lord Wellington becomes Duke of Wellington

August, British burn Washington

24 December, Treaty of Ghent ends war of 1812

1815   1 March, Napoleon leaves Elba, enters Paris 20 March

18 June, Battle of Waterloo, Wellington, and Blucher defeat Napoleon

1819   United States purchases Florida from Spain; Singapore founded

1820   29 January, death of George III, George IV ascends throne (–1830)

1821   Hudson's Bay Company and North-West Company amalgamate

Greek War of Independence begins

1822   Brazil becomes independent

Liberia founded

1823   2 December, U.S. proclaims Monroe Doctrine, closing North and South America to colonial settlement by European powers

1828   Test Act repealed; dissenters could become MPs

1829   Catholic emancipation in U.K.

1830   26 June, death of George IV, succeeded by William IV (–1837)

July, revolution in France, Louis Philippe succeeds Charles X

1831 Bristol riots after defeat of first and second Reform Bills

Greece gains independence from the Ottoman Empire

1832 4 June, Reform Bill passed in House of Lords

1833 Upper Canada allows nonconformist clergy to perform marriages

1834 Civil war breaks out in Spain

British Houses of Parliament destroyed by fire

Abolition of slavery in all British possessions (see 1807)

1837 20 June, death of William IV, succeeded by Queen Victoria

1837–38 Rebellions in both Upper and Lower Canada

1838 First Afghan War

Public Record Office established

1839 Anglo-Chinese Opium War begins (–1842)

1840 10 February, Queen Victoria marries Prince Albert of Saxe-Coburg-Gotha

1841 10 February, Act of Union proclaimed, Upper and Lower Canada united as the Province of Canada, with a single legislature; Lower Canada (Quebec) termed Canada East, Upper Canada (Ontario), Canada West

Second Afghan War begins (–1842)

Hong Kong ceded by China to Great Britain

1842 Treaty of Nanking; China's cessation of Hong Kong to Britain confirmed

1843   Britain annexes Natal and Sind (India)

Free Church of Scotland formed

1844   Government of the Canadas moves from Kingston to Montreal

1845   U.S. annexes Texas

John Franklin expedition seeking North-West Passage sets out

Much of Irish potato crop destroyed by fungus, start of famine

1846   23 May, Repeal of the Corn Laws, eliminating colonial preferences

1847   Mormons found Salt Lake City

1848   February, France, abdication of Louis Philippe, republic proclaimed

10 December, Louis Napoleon elected President of French Republic

1849   13 January, Hudson's Bay Company granted trade monopoly on Vancouver Island; rights revoked 30 May 1858

25 April, Montreal, Parliament Houses burned to protest Rebellion Losses Bill

Gold Rush in California

Britain annexes the Punjab

1851   Great Exhibition & Crystal Palace

December, France, Louis Napoleon declared Emperor Napoleon III

Gold found in Australia

1853	4 October, Turkey declares war on Russia, Crimean War begins
1854	France and Britain declare war on Russia
	14 September, Allied forces land in Crimea
	Jews allowed to become MPs in U.K.
1856	30 March, Treaty of Paris ends Crimean War
1857	10 May, Sepoy revolt, start of Indian Mutiny
1858	Powers of East India Company transferred to British Crown
1859	War of Italian Liberation begins
1860	7 September, Garibaldi enters Naples
	26 October, Victor Emanuel proclaimed King of Italy
1861	4 March, Abraham Lincoln becomes President of U.S.
	American Civil War begins, Battle of Bull Run on 21 July
	August, Colony of British Columbia (mainland) established
	14 December, death of Prince Consort (Prince Albert)
1862	22 September, Lincoln declares all slaves will be free on 1 January 1863
1865	9 April, Robert E. Lee surrenders at Appomattox
	14 April, Lincoln assassinated by J.W. Booth
	26 May, Last Confederate army surrenders, end of Civil War

1866   Fenian Raids at Fort Erie (Canada West), Pigeon Hill (Canada East)

17 November, Colony of Vancouver Island annexed to British Columbia

1867   1 July, Confederation; British North America Act establishes the Dominion of Canada with New Brunswick, Nova Scotia, Ontario, and Quebec

U.S. acquires Alaska from Russia

1870   11 May, Dominion of Canada pays Hudson's Bay Company £300,000 for Rupert's Land

23 June, Rupert's Land becomes the Northwest Territories

1870   15 July, Manitoba made province of Canada in the Manitoba Act

Franco-Prussian war begins

19 September, Seige of Paris begins

1871   German Empire established, William I of Prussia made Emperor

28 January, France and Germany sign armistice

March–May, Commune rising in Paris

Treaty of Washington, British forces leave most of Canada

20 July, British Columbia joins Canada under the British Columbia Terms of Union

1873   1 July, Prince Edward Island joins Canada under the Prince Edward Island Terms of Union

1877   1 January, Queen Victoria proclaimed Empress of India

1880   Transvaal Boers proclaim a Republic in southern Africa, hostilities ensue leading to the First Boer War

1881   April, Britain recognizes independence of Transvaal Republic

1885   Standard Time implemented worldwide; developed by Sir Sandford Fleming (1827–1915) in Canada

1892   Famine in Russia

1894   Uganda becomes a British Protectorate

1895   Massacre of Armenians in Constantinople

1898   The Yukon Act makes Yukon a separate territory

Spanish-American war, Spain loses Cuba, Puerto Rico and Philippines

1899   October, Second Boer War begins

1900   Boxer Rising in China

1901   Australia becomes a dominion

22 January, death of Queen Victoria, succeeded by Edward VII (–1910)

1902   9 June, South African Boers sign terms of surrender at Pretoria

1905   Alberta and Saskatchewan become provinces of Canada

1906   19 April, San Francisco earthquake and fire

1910   6 May, death of Edward VII, George V ascends throne (–1936)

July, Union of South Africa becomes a dominion

August, Japan annexes Korea

1912   15/16 April, Titanic sinks

Boundaries of Manitoba, Ontario, and Quebec expand to their present limits, North-West Territories reduced accordingly

1914   28 June, assassination of Archduke Franz Ferdinand in Sarajevo

28 July, Austria declares war on Serbia

1 August, Germany declares war on Russia

3 August, Germany declares war on France

4 August, England declares war on Germany and vice versa

1915   22 April, Anglo-French forces land at Gallipoli

23 May, Italy declares war on Germany and Austria-Hungary

1916   23 April, Easter Rising in Dublin

1917   Revolution in Russia, Nicholas II abdicates

6 April, U.S. enters war against Germany

9–13 April, Battle of Vimy Ridge

26 June, U.S. Forces land in France

October, Bolshevik coup d'état in Russia

6 November, Canadians capture Passchendale Ridge

November, Balfour Declaration on Palestine

December, Germany and Russia sign Armistice at Brest-Litovsk

1918   16–17 July, Russian Royal family murdered by

Bolsheviks

11 November, Germany signs Armistice at Compiègne, end of First World War

1919   Nickel Resolution bans British honours bearing titles in Canada

21 January, Irish Free State proclaimed

1920   10 January, League of Nations founded

1921   6 December, Anglo-Irish treaty establishes the Irish Free State

1923   1 January, Union of Soviet Socialist Republics (U.S.S.R.) formed

1926   May, General Strike in Britain

15 May–25 June, Winnipeg General Strike

1927   Quebec-Labrador boundary defined by the Judicial Committee of the Privy Council in Great Britain

1932   F.D. Roosevelt elected to the office of president of the U.S.; takes office in 1933

1933   30 January, Hitler becomes German Chancellor

1936   20 January, death of George V, Edward VIII succeeds to throne

10–11 December, Edward VIII abdicates, George VI succeeds (–1952)

17 July, Spanish Civil War begins

1937   26 April, Spain, Guernica destroyed by German bombers

December, Japanese forces take Nanking

1938   30 September, Munich Agreement, Sudaten-
land given to Germany

9–10 November, *Kristallnacht* (Germany, anti-
Jewish riots)

1939   Collapse of Republican resistance in Spain

March, Germany occupies Czechoslovakia

1 September, Germany invades Poland

3 September, Britain and France declare war on
Nazi Germany

10 September, Canada declares war on
Germany

28 September, Germany and Russia partition
Poland

1940   April, Germany invades Norway and Denmark

May, Germany invaded Netherlands and
France

27 May, evacuation of Dunkirk begins

10 June, Italy enters war against England,
France, and Canada

22 June, German French Armistice signed

July–September, Battle of Britain

1941   22 June, Germany invades Russia, seige of
Leningrad begins 8 September.

7 December, Japanese attack Pearl Harbor

11 December, Germany and Italy declare war
on the U.S.

1942   15 February, Singapore surrenders to Japanese

19 August, Dieppe Raid

4 November, British victory at El Alamein

1943   18 January, the 17-month siege of Stalingrad is broken

10 July, Allied troops arrive in occupied Sicily

1944   6 June, D Day, Allies invade Europe

24 August, Liberation of Paris

1945   4–11 February, Churchill, Roosevelt, and Stalin meet at Yalta

12 April, death of F.D. Roosevelt, Harry Truman becomes president

2 May, fall of Berlin; 8 May, Germany surrenders

6–9 August, Atomic bombs dropped on Hiroshima and Nagasaki

2 September, Japan surrenders

1946   10 January, first meeting of United Nations General Assembly

1947   1 January, Canadian Citizenship Act comes into force

June, Partition of India announced

1948   May, British Mandate in Palestine ends, State of Israel created

June, Berlin airlift begins, ends May 1949

1949   Newfoundland and Labrador join Confederation

Declaration of London, Commonwealth founded

1950   6 June, Korean War begins

1952   6 February, death of George VI, Elizabeth II

ascends to the throne

1956   July–November, Suez Crisis

October, Abortive Hungarian revolution begins

1959   February, Fidel Castro takes power in Cuba

1962   July, Algerian independence from France

1963   22 November, John F. Kennedy assassinated

1965   March, U.S. Marines land in South Vietnam, start of Vietnam War

1966   Cultural Revolution begins in China

1967   June, Arab–Israeli Six Day War

1971   War in Pakistan, East Pakistan becomes Bangladesh

1973   January, U.S., North and South Vietnam sign cease fire in Paris

March, last U.S. troops leave Vietnam

1974   July, Turkey invades Cyprus

1975   20 November, death of Franco, monarchy restored in Spain

1979   January, Iranian revolution, Shah and family flee

December, Russia invades Afghanistan

1980   April, Rhodesia becomes independent, renamed Zimbabwe

4 May, death of President Tito of Yugoslavia

1982   19 March–14 June, Falklands War

1988   May, Russia withdraws from Afghanistan

1989   November, Fall of the Berlin Wall

1991   January–March, Gulf War

           May, Civil war in Yugoslavia begins

1993   1 January, Czechoslovakia divides into separate
           Czech and Slovakian Republics

1997   1 July, Britain transfers Hong Kong back to
           China

1998   19 November, Scotland Act receives royal
           assent, Scottish Parliament restored after some
           290 years (see 1707)

1999   The Nunavut Act makes Nunavut a separate
           Territory

2001   9 September, Attack on World Trade Centre in
           New York

           Latest Afghan war begins, Kabul liberated in
           November (see 1838, 1841)

2003   19 March, U.S. and U.K. declare war on Iraq

For full details of any Canadian event, consult *The Fitzhenry & Whiteside Book of Canadian Facts & Dates*, for worldwide chronologies of historical and scientific events see *The Oxford Encyclopedic English Dictionary*.

Notes

Chapter 1 — A Time Traveller's Frame of Reference

1. A partial digital text can be found on Google Books (*http://books.google.ca*) under the title, *Technological Revolutions and Financial Capital.*

2. Institute of Electrical and Electronic Engineers, *IEEE Canadian Review* (Spring, 2006): 18.

3. T. H. Raddall, *In My Time: A Memoir* (Toronto: McClelland & Stewart, 1976), 154–55.

4. Juliet Nicolson, *The Perfect Summer* (London: John Murray, 2006). Of course you could also get the DVDs and watch the 68 episodes of *Upstairs, Downstairs.*

5. Michael J. Smith and William P. Angley, *The McCoy Printing Company Picture Postcard Handbook 1900– 1910* (published by the authors, 2009), 10.

6. Witold Rybczynski, *Home: A Short History of an Idea* (Markham, ON: Penguin Books Canada Ltd., 1987), 138.

7. Based in part on a review in *The Economist*, Vol. 391, No. 8632 (May 23–29, 2009) of Robert C. Allen, *The British Industrial Revolution in Global Perspective* (Cambridge, U.K.: Cambridge University Press, 2009).

8. The foundations of the first cotton mill in Manchester were hidden under a car park at the University of Manchester, and were excavated by the BBC's *Time Team* in September 2005.

9   Daniel Pool, *What Jane Austen Ate and Charles Dickens Knew: From Fox Hunting to Whist — the Facts of Daily Life in 19th-Century England* (New York: Temple Books, Simon & Schuster Inc., 1994).

Chapter 2 — Dealing with Documents

1. Patricia Kennedy explains how the "pyramid of power" and "reporting relationships" influence the content of records in "Approaching an Iceberg," *Canadian State Trials: Law, Politics, and Security Measures, 1608–1837*, ed. F. Murray Greenwood and Barry Wright (Toronto: University of Toronto Press, 1996), Appendix 1.

2. Patricia Kennedy has studied the various versions of Ontario's U.E. List. In *How to Trace Your Loyalist Ancestors* (Ottawa: Ottawa Branch OGS, 1989), 7–9, she discusses the reliability of such government records, how variants occurred, and how to decide which to accept. Her lesson is universal, and not confined to would-be U.E.s.

3. Brenda Merriman, *Genealogy in Ontario: Searching the Records* (Toronto: The Ontario Genealogical Society, 2008).

4. Michael E. Fitton, "It Is Written," *Families*, Vol.48, No.4 (Nov. 2009): 26–28.

Chapter 3 — Dealing with Family Tradition

1. George Maclean Rose, ed., *A Cyclopedia of Canadian Biography: Being Chiefly Men of the Time*, (Toronto: Rose Publishing Co., 1888), 263.

2. *Biographical Review this volume contains biographical sketches of leading citizens of the province of New Brunswick under the editorial supervision of I. Allen Jack* I. Allen Jack, Q.C., ed. (Boston, Biographical Review Publishing Company, 1900), 34–37.

Chapter 4 —What Every Schoolchild Used to Know

1. Government brochure, *The Metric Traveller*, Transport Canada, Road Safety, (no date).

2. The medieval origins of some of these measures along with many other obsolete terms can be found in the first section of John Richardson's *The Local Historian's Encyclopedia* (New Barnet, Herts, England: Historical Publications Ltd., 1974, 4th revised reprint, 1983), 9–35.

3. E.M. Kirkpatrick ed., *Chambers 20th Century Dictionary* (Edinburgh: Chambers, new edition, 1983).

4. *The American College Dictionary* (New York: Random House, 1948).

5. Michael E. Marlatt, "French Measurements," *The Beaver*, (April–May, 1998): 46, citing the work of Conrad Heidenreich, published in *The Canadian Cartographer* Vol. 12, No. 2 (1972).

6. See Patricia Kennedy, "The Measures of Trade," *The Archivist*, Vol. 20, No. 2 (1994): 5–8.

7. Ibid., 8: note 3.

8. Horace Doursther, *Dictionnaire universel des poids* (1840, reprinted 1965).

9. Stella Tillyard, *Aristocrats: Carolyn, Emily, Louisa and Sarah Lennox 1740–1832* (Chatto & Windus Ltd., 1994; Vintage, 1995), 7.

Chapter 5 — Money

1. Margaret Thatcher in the *Observer*, 18 November 1979.

2. Large cents were minted until 1920 and were in circulation for several decades after that. They were copper or bronze and 25.40 millimetres in diameter.

Image Courtesy of Ruth Chernia.

3. *Encyclopedia Britannica,* 11th edition,1906.

4. Ibid.

5. *Oxford Encyclopedic English Dictionary* (Oxford: Oxford University Press, 1991).

Chapter 6 — The Value of Money

1. A description of these *Sessional Papers,* with suggestions on how to use them, is found in Althea Douglas, *Canadian Railway Records: A Guide for Genealogists — Revised and Expanded* (Toronto: Ontario Genealogical Society, 2004), 66–70.

2. *Sessional Papers 1909* (Vol. XLII), paper No.1: "The Auditor General's Report, 1907–1908," Part W "Railways and Canals Department," under "Expenditures," W-223, W-201.

3. G. de T. Glazebrook, Katharine B. Brett and Judith McErvell, eds., *Eaton's Catalogues 1886–1930* (Toronto: University of Toronto Press, 1969). The Introduction and preliminary essays have added data on wages and housing costs.

4. *The Ordanance Survey Atlas of Great Britain* (Southampton & Feltham, Middlesex: Ordnance Survey & Country Life Books, 1982) and *Oxford Encyclopedic English Dictionary.*

5. Wages and prices are taken from Thorold Rogers, *A History of Prices and Agriculture in England* (Oxford, 1866).

6. Stella Tillyard, *Aristocrats: Carolyn, Emily, Louisa and Sarah Lennox 1740–1832* (Chatto & Windus Ltd., 1994; Vintage, 1995), 7–8.

7. James Boswell, *Boswell's London Journal 1762–1763*, Frederick A. Pottle, ed (Toronto: McGraw-Hill Book Co., Inc., 1950), 304–5.

8. Ibid., 336–7.

9. Janet Gleeson, *Privilege & Scandal: The Remarkable Life of Harriet Spencer, Sister of Georgiana* (New York: Three Rivers Press, 2006), 26.

10. The biographer and critic, Lord David Cecil (1902–1986), details many of these subtleties in the introductory chapters to his biographies of Jane Austen and William Lamb, Lord Melbourne.

11. Lord David Cecil, *A Portrait of Jane Austen* (Penguin Books, 1980), 109.

12. Jane Austin, *Pride and Prejudice* (London: The Folio Society, 2006), 14.

13. Jane Austin, *Sense and Sensibility* (New York: Penguin Group (USA) Inc., 1997), 239.

14. Charlotte Brontë, *Jane Eyre* (London: Collins Clear Type Press, no date), 430.

15. Francis (Fanny) Burney, *The Journals and Letters of Fanny Burney (Madame d'Arblay)*, Joyce Hemow, with Althea Douglas and Patricia Hawkins, eds. (Oxford: Clarendon Press, Vols. XI and XII, 1984), Vol. XII, 978.

16. Ibid., 41.

17. Ibid., Vol. XI, 688.

18. Tag line from a song written by Don Wolvin for the McGill *Red and White Revue* of 1948 or 1949.

Chapter 7 — Travel in the Past

1. Jane Austen, *Pride and Prejudice* (London: The Folio Society, 2006), 169.

2. Christopher Andreae with Geoffrey Matthews, *Lines of Country: An Atlas of Railway and Waterway History in Canada* (Erin, ON: The Boston Mills Press, 1997) and Dominion Bureau of Statistics, *Canada 1934: The Official Handbook of Present Conditions and Recent Progress* (Ottawa: Department of Trade and Commerce, 1934).

3. Jane Ellice, *The Diary of June Ellice*, Patricia Godsell, ed. (Ottawa: Oberon Press, 1975), 18, 31, 159, 167.

4. Stanley T. Spicer, *Maritimers Ashore & Afloat* (Hantsport, NS: Lancelot Press, Vol.1, 1993; Vol.2, 1994), 1,103.

5. Dr. C. Sotheby Pitcher, "A Voyage to China in 1806," *Family Tree Magazine* (Aug. 1997): 8–10.

6. Marian Fowler, *Below the Peacock Fan: First Ladies of the Raj* (New York: Penguin Books Ltd., 1987), 22, 24.

7. Ibid, 104–105.

8. Ibid, 256.

9. D. Housby, comp., *Representative Books of the Last 100 Years 1883–1983* (Toronto: Toronto Public Library, 1983), 14.

10. Spicer, *Maritimers*, 1,107.

11. Daniel Pool, *What Jane Austen Ate and Charles Dickens Knew: From Fox Hunting to Whist — the Facts of Daily Life in 19th-Century England* (New York: Temple Books, Simon & Schuster Inc., 1994), 143.

12. Jane Austen, *Persuasion* (Mineola, New York: Dover Publications Inc., 1997), 69–70.

13. J.B. Snell, *Early Railways* (London: Weidenfeld and Nicholson, 1964, 1967), 22.

14. These trials were a locomotive competition set up by the Liverpool and Manchester Railway to determine which steam engine could meet rather stringent conditions. Robert Stephenson's Rocket was the only one to fulfill the terms.

15. Hamilton Ellis, *The Pictorial Encyclopedia of Railways* (Feltham, Middlesex: The Hamlyn Publishing group, Ltd., 1968), 38.

16. *http://en.wikipedia.org/wiki/Greyhound_Lines* (accessed 6 October 2010).

17. *Canada 1934*, 121.

18. *Historical Atlas of Canada, Volume I*, R. Cole Harris ed.(1987); *Volume II*, R. Louis Gentilcore *et al.* eds. (1993); *Volume III*, Donald Kerr ed. (1990). Designer

and cartographer Geoffrey J. Matthews. (Toronto: University of Toronto Press, 3 Vols.).

19. Charlotte Gray, "First Flight," *The Beaver: Canada's History Magazine* (Feb./ March 2009): 18–19.

20. Juliet Nicolson, *The Perfect Summer* (London: John Murray, 2006), 127, 249.

21. *Canada 1934*, 122.

Chapter 8 — Trades and Their Tools

1. *The Boy's Book of Trades and the Tools Used in Them* (Ottawa: Algrove Publishing Ltd., 1999, reprinted from the edition first published London: New York; G. Routledge and Sons, 1866), Preface.

2. Both definitions are from the *Oxford Encyclopedic English Dictionary*.

3. N.W. Kay, ed. *The Practical Carpenter and Joiner, Illustrated* (London: Odhams Press Ltd., n.d.), 2, 14.

4. *The Boy's Book*, 57.

5. Ibid., 45.

6. Ibid., 56.

7. Ibid., 64.

8. Ibid., 98.

9. Ibid., 224.

10. Ibid., 246.

11. Ibid., 233.

12. "The Log-Driver's Waltz" is a traditional folk song by Wade Hemsworth. It was sung in an animated film of the same title, which was made by the National Film Board.

13. *Saint John Daily Telegraph*, Morning Edition, (25 June 1872): 3.

14. The Saint John *Daily News*, (22 November 1876), lists the names of those lost.

15. The complete registers of ships built in Canada are available on microfilm from Library and Archives Canada; see also Chapter 16 (Our Seafaring and Military heritage). Note that the searchable database of Shipping Registers covers only 10 ports in Atlantic Canada.

16. Ibid.

17. Ibid.

Chapter 9 — Work Away From Home

1. Charles Kingsley, "The Three Fishers," *Shorter Poems Revised Edition*, selected by W.J. Alexander, Professor of English Literature, University College Toronto (Toronto: The T. Eaton Co. Limited, 1924), 299. The poem was first published 1858.

2. Rudyard Kipling, "The Explorer," *Collected Verse of Rudyard Kipling* (New York: Doubleday, Page & Company, 1919), 19. The poem was first published 1898.

3. Hughson and Bond's *Hurling Down the Pine* (Chelsea, QC: Historical Society of the Gatineau, 1964, 3rd ed.

1987) gives a vivid description of life in the shanties, as well as a detailed history of the timber trade on the Ottawa and Gatineau Rivers.

4. See Althea Douglas, *Canadian Railway Records* (Toronto: Ontario Genealogical Society, 2004), 66–70.

5. Melynda Jarratt, *War Brides: The Stories of the Women Who Left Everything Behind to Follow the Men They Loved* (Toronto: Dundurn Press, 2009).

6. Pier 21, Halifax, Nova Scotia, *www.pier21.ca.*

7. Jessica Mann, *Out Of Harm's Way. The Wartime Evacuation of Children from Britain* (London, U.K.: Headline Book Publishing, 2005).

8. James Morrison, *Aboriginal People in the Archives: A Guide to Sources in the Archives of Ontario* (Toronto: Ministry of Culture and Communication, 1982), 20.

9. Bill Russell, *Records of the Department of Indian Affairs at Library and Archives Canada,* 2nd edition (Toronto: Ontario Genealogical Society, 2004), 76.

10. Anthony J. Camp, *My Ancestors Moved in England or Wales* (London: Society of Genealogists, 1994), 8. This handbook is well worth studying even if your migrants did not originate in England or Wales.

Chapter 10 — Family and Connections

1. Roger D. Masters, *The Nature of Politics* (New Haven & London: Yale University Press, 1989). Discussing the "survival of the fittest," defined fitness is as the

capacity to transmit genes to succeeding generations (6). Various authorities and opinions on the numbers in a kinship group are given, 219.

2. Stella Colwell, "Family History into Community History," *Genealogists' Magazine*, Vol. 24, No. 6 (June 1993): 247.

3. Naomi Griffith, *The Contexts of Acadian History, 1686–1784* (Montreal, Kingston: McGill-Queen's University Press, 1992), 17.

4. Anthony J. Camp, "Your Average Ancestor," *Family Tree Magazine* (Aug. 2001): 12–13.

5. Daniel Pool, *What Jane Austen Ate and Charles Dickens Knew: From Fox Hunting to Whist — the Facts of Daily Life in 19th-Century England* (New York: Temple Books, Simon & Schuster Inc., 1994), 187.

6. Jean Noble, "It's A Wise Child …," *Family Tree Magazine* Vol. 11, No. 12 (Oct. 1995): 4–5.

7. Lord David Cecil, *Melbourne* (New York: Charter Books, 1962), 21.

8. Janet Gleeson, *Privilege & Scandal: The Remarkable Life of Harriet Spencer, Sister of Georgiana* (New York: Three Rivers Press, 2006), 270n.

9. Henriette-Lucy Dillon, La Tour du Pin, *Memoirs of Madame de La Tour du Pin*, ed. and trans. Felice Harcourt (New York: The McCall Publishing Company, 1971), 83.

10. Juliet Nicolson, *The Perfect Summer* (London: John Murray, 2006), 84–7.

11. Stella Tillyard, *Aristocrats: Carolyn, Emily, Louisa and Sarah Lennox 1740–1832* (Chatto & Windus Ltd., 1994; Vintage, 1995), 281.

12. Pool, *What Jane Austen Ate and Charles Dickens Knew*, 230.

13. Camp, "Your Average Ancestor," 13.

14. Anthony Hopkins, *Songs from the Front & Rear; Canadian Servicemen's Songs of the Second World War* (Edmonton: Hurtig Publishers, 1979), 8.

15. Ibid., 9.

16. Gertrude Pringle, *Etiquette in Canada: The Blue Book of Social Usage* (Toronto: McClelland & Stewart 1932, 2nd ed. 1949), 371.

17. Ibid., 376.

18. Ibid., 377.

Chapter 11 — Home Sweet Home

1. *Encyclopædia Britannica*, 1911.

2. Recent studies of nineteenth-century health and sanitation include Steven Johnson's *The Ghost Map The Story of London's Most Terrifying Epidemic — and How It Changed Science, Cities, and the Modern World* (New York: Riverhead Books, 2006) and Michael Bliss, *Plague: A Story of Smallpox in Montreal* (Toronto: HarperCollins Publishers, Ltd., 1991).

3. Francis Burney, *The Journals and Letters of Fanny Burney (Madame d'Arblay)*, Joyce Hemlow, George G. Falle, Althea Douglas and Jill A. Bourdais de Charbonnière, eds., Vol. V (Oxford: Clarendon Press, 1975), 234, 255.

4. For descriptions of housing, see David P. Jordan, *Transforming Paris: The Life and Labours of Baron Haussmann* (New York: The Free Press/Simon & Shuster, 1995), 291–295.

5. Isabelle Gournay and France Vanlaethem, eds., *Montreal Metropolis 1880–1930* (Toronto: Stoddard Publishing for the Canadian Centre for Architecture, 1998), 162. This is an informative study of urban architecture and lifestyles to 1930.

Chapter 12 — How We Lived Then

1. For a fuller discussion of basic inventions, see J.G. Landels, *Engineering in the Ancient World* (Berkley and Los Angeles: University of California Press, 1978).

2. *Oxford Encyclopedic English Dictionary.*

3. *Encyclopædia Britannica*, 1911.

4. Ibid.

5. *Encyclopedia Britannica*, 1946.

6. Witold Rybczynski, *Home: A Short History of an Idea* (Markham, ON: Penguin Books Canada Ltd., 1986), 151.

7. *Oxford Encyclopedic English Dictionary*, 461.

8. Dominion Bureau of Statistics, *Canada 1934: The Official Handbook of Present Conditions and Recent Progress* (Ottawa: Department of Trade and Commerce, 1934), 103.

9. Ibid, 104.

10. Juliet Nicolson, *The Perfect Summer* (London: John Murray, 2006), 155.

11. Rybczynski, *Home*,152.

12. Ibid., 157.

13. Camilla Bonn, "1996 And All That a Chronicle of British Identity," *Country Life*, Vol. CXC, no. 5 (1 Feb. 1996): 38–39.

14. "Young Ladies' Aid" of St. John's United Church, *Y.L.A. Recipes* (Moncton, NB: 1948), 11.

15. *Wise Encyclopedia of Cookery* (New York: Wm. H. Wise & Co. Inc., 1948), 955.

16. Ibid., 515.

17. "Living in the global goldfish bowl," *The Economist*, Vol. 353, No. 8150 (18 Dec. 1999): 51, col.1.

Chapter 13 — Health in the Past

1. Arnold Bennett, *The Card: A Story of Adventure in the Five Towns* (1913) as quoted in *The Oxford Dictionary of Thematic Quotations*, Susan Ratcliffe, ed. (Oxford: Oxford University Press, 2000), 350.

Chapter 14 — Our Heritage

1. "The Lion and the Unicorn," *Lavender's Blue: A Book of Nursery Rhymes,* Kathleen Lines, compiler (London: Oxford University Press, 1967), 80–81. The *Oxford Dictionary of Quotations* (page 567) gives as the original source "MS inscription (c.1691) beside a woodcut of the royal arms in a bible in the Opie Collection," their source being William King, *Useful Transactions in Philosophy* (1707–9).

2. R.S. Longley, "The Coming of the New England Planters to the Annapolis Valley," *They Planted Well,* Margaret Conrad, ed. (Fredericton, NB: Acadiensis Press, 1988), 16.

3. *Historical Atlas of Canada III*, Plate 34, G.J. Matthews has drawn a pedigree chart illustrating "The Road to Church Union."

4. Ruth Ortego Berthelot, ed., *Early Notaries of Canada With an Introduction by René Chartrand* (New Orleans: Polyanthos, 1977). The English introduction gives a brief outline of the profession in early Quebec. The French text consists of chronologically arranged biographies of notaries, with indexes to names and places. For a brief outline of French colonial administration and the role of the notary see the *Dictionary of Canadian Biography*, general editor David M. Hayne (Toronto: University of Toronto Press, Vol. II, 1969), André Vachon, "The Administration of New France," xv–xxv.

5. For an extensive reading list on the profession, see John P. DuLong, Ph.D., "French Canadian and Acadian

Notarial Records," a bibliography, published in *Proceedings O.G.S. Seminar '95* (Chatham, ON: OGS, 1995), 126–127.

Chapter 15 — Our VIP Heritage

1. Thomas H. Raddall, *Halifax: Warden of the North* (Toronto: McClelland & Stewart, 1948), 22.

2. Ibid., 43.

3. Jobb, Dean, "'The first that was ever publish'd in the Province': John Bushell's *Halifax Gazette*, 1752–1761," *Royal Nova Scotia Historical Society Journal*, Vol. 11, (2008): 1.

4. Chris Raible, "'A Printer is Indispensably Necessary' The tribulations of Canada's earliest printers," *The Beaver*, Vol. 77, No. 4 (Aug./Sept. 1997): 19.

5. Ibid.: 24.

6. A lively account of one such politically based editorial rivalry is given by John Edward Belliveau, "Hawke of the *Transcript*: A forgotten hero of Canadian journalism," *The Beaver*, Vol. 77:4 (August/September 1997): 35–37.

7. *Chambers 20th Century Dictionary*, E.M. Kirkpatrick, ed. (Edinburgh: Chambers. New edition, 1983).

8. For a fuller description of available indexes see: Althea Douglas, "The indexes of 18th and early 19th-century magazines," *The Indexer*, Vol. 14, No. 3 (April 1985): 160–63.

Chapter 16 — Our Seafaring and Military Heritage

1. See *Historical Atlas of Canada, Vol.II*, Plate 24 "British Garrisons to 1871."

2. Sheila Kindred, "James Cook: Cartographer in the Making, 1758–1762" *Royal Nova Scotia Historical Society Journal*, Vol.12 (2009): 54–81.

3. Thomas H. Raddall, *Halifax: Warden of the North* (Toronto: McClelland & Stewart, 1948), 63.

4. Sheila Kindred, "Jane Austen's Naval Brother Charles on the North American Station 1805–1811," *Royal Nova Scotia Historical Society Journal*, Vol.10 (2007): 25.

5. Raddall, *Halifax*, 142.

6. Ibid., 244–45.

7. Charles A. Armour and Thomas Lackey, *Sailing Ships of the Maritimes: An Illustrated History of Shipping and Shipbuilding in the Maritime Provinces of Canada 1750–1925*, (Toronto etc.: McGraw-Hill Ryerson Ltd.,1975), 118.

8. Armour, *Sailing Ships*, (214–215) and W.E.F. Ward, *The Royal Navy and the Slavers: The Suppression of the Atlantic Slave Trade* (New York: Schocken Books, 1970), 25–28; 232–239.

9. Roberta Thomas, "The Maritime History Archive, Memorial University of Newfoundland: sources for research" *Families*, Vol. 34, No. 1 (February 1995): 5–13.

10. Esther Clark Wright, *The Ships of St. Martins* (Saint John: New Brunswick Museum, 1974, reprinted 1978), 12.

11. *Oxford Encyclopedic English Dictionary.*

12. Raddall, *Halifax*, 124.

13. Mary K. MacLeod, *Whisper in the Air: Marconi The Canadian Years, 1902–1946* (Hantsport, NS: Lancelot Press, 1992), 39.

14. Margaret Cheney, *Tesla: Man out of Time* (New York: Dell Publishing, 1981), 84.

15. For a full account of the early Marconi years see: Mary K. MacLeod, *Whisper in the Air*. Library and Archives Canada have the Canadian Marconi Co. archives, however very little early material has survived. The British Marconi Company had archives at Chelmsford.

16. Thomas H. Raddall, *In My Time: A Memoir* (McClellend & Stewart, 1977), 117.

17. N.A.M. Rodger, *Naval Records for Genealogists* (London: Public Record Office, 1984).

18. Ibid., 5.

19. Kindred, "James Cook": 54.

20. Ibid., 72: note 2.

21. To commemorate the centennial, Dundurn Press has published *The Naval Service of Canada, 1910–2010*, and *La marine du Canada, 1910–2010*, ed. Richard H. Gimblett. Contributions by 12 recognized authorities

and a wealth of illustrations, maps, charts and a bibli-ography make it a valuable research source.

22. Raddall, *Halifax*, 245.

23. Ibid., 255.

24. Hopkins, 74.

25. Ibid., 100.

Bibliography

Standard Reference Works

The American College Dictionary, Clarence L. Barnhardt, ed. New York: Random House, second printing, 1948.

Chambers 20th Century Dictionary, E.M. Kirkpatrick, ed. Edinburgh: Chambers, new edition, 1983.

Chambers Biographical Dictionary, Magnus Magnusson KBE, ed. Edinburgh, New York: Chambers, fifth edition, 1990.

The Encyclopædia Britannica; A Dictionary of Arts, Sciences, Literature and General Information: Eleventh Edition, New York: The Encyclopædia Britannica Company, 1910–11.

Encyclopædia Britannica: A New Survey of Universal Knowledge. Fourteenth Edition, Chicago, London, Toronto: University of Chicago, 1946.

Oxford Encyclopedic English Dictionary, Joyce M. Hawkins and Robert Allen, eds. Oxford: Clarendon Press, 1991.

The Ordnance Survey Atlas of Great Britain Southampton & Feltham Middlesex: Ordnance Survey & Country Life Books, 1982.

Sources Consulted and/or Cited

Abrahamson, Roy A., comp. *Selections from Almanacks of Early Canada*. Toronto: Cherry Tree Press, 1982.

Andreae, Christopher with Geoffrey Matthews. *Lines of Country: An Atlas of Railway and waterway History in Canada*. Erin, ON: The Boston Mills Press, 1997.

Armour, Charles A., and Thomas Lackey. *Sailing Ships of the Maritimes: An Illustrated History of Shipping and Shipbuilding in the Maritime Provinces of Canada 1750–1925*. Toronto etc.: McGraw-Hill Ryerson Ltd.,1975.

_____ with additions by Allan D. Smith. *Shipbuilding in Westmorland County New Brunswick 1784–1910*. Sackville, NB: Tantramar Heritage Trust, 2008.

Austen, Jane. *Northanger Abbey*. Ware, Herfordshire: Wordsworth Editions Limited, 1993.

_____. *Persuasion*. Mineola, New York: Dover Publications, Inc., 1997

_____. *Pride and Prejudice*. London: The Folio Society, 2006.

_____. *Sense and Sensibility*. New York: Penguin Group (USA) Inc., 1997.

Baird, Donal. *Women at Sea in the Age of Sail*. Halifax, NS: Nimbus Publishing, 2001.

Berthelot, Ruth Ortego, ed. *Early Notaries of Canada with an Introductin by René Chartrand*. New Orleans: Polyanthos, 1977.

Bliss, Michael. *Plague: A Story of Smallpox in Montreal*. Toronto: Harper Collins Publishers Ltd., 1991.

Bonn, Camilla. "1996 And All That a Chronicle of British Identity," *Country Life*, Vol.CXC, No.5 (1 Feb. 1996), 38–39.

Boswell, James. *Boswell's London Journal 1762–1763*. Frederick A. Pottle, ed. New York, London, Toronto: McGraw-Hill Book Co., Inc., 1950.

The Boy's Book of Trades and the Tools Used in Them. Ottawa: Algrove Publishing Ltd., 1999, Reprinted from the edition first published: London, New York: George Routledge and Sons, 1866. [no author or editor]

Briggs, Elizabeth. *A Family Historian's Guide to Illness, Disease & Death Certificates*. Toronto: Ontario Genealogical Society, 1993.

Bronte, Charlotte. *Jane Eyre*. London: Collins Clear Type Press, no date.

Burney, Frances (Fanny), *The Journals and Letters of Fanny Burney (Madame d'Arblay)*. General editor Joyce Hemlow, Oxford: Clarendon Press, 12 vols. 1972-1984.

Vol. V, Hemlow with George G. Falle, Althea Douglas and Jill A. Bourdais de Charbonnière, 1975; Vols. XI and XII, ed. Hemlow with Althea Douglas and Patricia Hawkins, 1984.

Camp, Anthony J. *My Ancestors Moved in England or Wales.* London: Society of Genealogists, 1994.

_____. "Your Average Ancestor." *Family Tree Magazine* (August 2001), 12–13.

Cecil, Lord David. *Melbourne.* New York: Charter Books, 1962.

_____. *A Portrait of Jane Austen.* London: Penguin Books, 1980.

Cheney, Margaret. *Tesla: Man out of Time.* New York, Dell Publishing, 1981.

Colwell, Stella. "Family History into Community History." *Genealogists' Magazine*, Vol.24, No.6 (June 1993), 246–250.

Cook, Terry. *Sources for the Study of the Canadian North.* Ottawa: Library and Archives Canada, 1980.

Crowe, John Congdon. *In The Days of the Windjammers.* Toronto: Ryerson Press, 1959.

Daniels, Roger. *Coming to America: A History of Immigration and Ethnicity in American Life.* New York: Harper Collins, 1991.

Darling, Ian. *Amazing Airmen: Canadian Flyers in the Second World War.* Toronto: Dundurn Press, 2009.

Dollfus, Audouin. "L'art et l'invention des ballons," *Revue du Palais de la Découvrte*, Vol. 12, No. 112 (November 1983), 17–42.

Dominion Bureau of Statistics. *Canada 1934: The Official Handbook of Present Conditions and Recent Progress.* Ottawa: Department of Trade and Commerce, 1934.

Douglas, Althea. *Here be Dragons, too! More Navigational Hazards for the Canadian Family Researcher.* Toronto: Ontario Genealogical Society, 2000.

_____. and Creighton J. Douglas, *Canadian Railway Records: A Guide for Genealogists, Revised and Expanded.* Toronto: Ontario Genealogical Society, 2004.

Doursther, Horace. *Dictionnaire universel des poids et measures anciens et modernes de tous les pays.* Published originally in 1840. Reprinted in Amsterdam: Meridian Publishing Co., 1965.

Ellis, Hamilton. *The Pictorial Encyclopedia of Railways.* Feltham, Middlesex: The Hamlyn Publishing Group, Ltd., 1968.

Ferguson, Niall. *The Ascent of Money: A Financial History of the World.* London: Penguin Books Ltd., 2008.

Filby, P. William. *American & British Genealogy & Heraldry: A Selected List of Books.* Chicago: American Library Association, 1970.

Fitton, Michael E. "It Is Written," *Families*, Vol.48, No.4 (November 2009), 26–28.

Fowler, Marian. *Below the Peacock Fan: First Ladies of the Raj.* London: Penguin Books Ltd., 1987.

Gimblett, Richard H., ed. *The Naval Service of Canada 1910–2010.* Toronto: Dundurn Press, 2009.

Glazebrook, G. de T., Katharine B. Bret, and Judith McErvel, eds. *Pages from Eaton's Catalogues 1886–1930, A Shopper's View of Canada's Past.* Toronto: University of Toronto Press, 1969.

Gleeson, Janet. *Privilege & Scandal: The Remarkable Life of Harriet Spencer, Sister of Georgiana.* New York: Three Rivers Press, 2006.

Glover, Thomas J. *Pocket Ref.* Second edition. Littleton, Colorado: Sequoia Publishing Inc., 1989–2000. Available through Lee Valley Tools Ltd.

Godsell, Patricia, ed. *The Diary of Jane Ellice.* Ottawa: Oberon Press, 1975.

Gournay, Isabelle and France Vanlaethem, eds. *Montreal Metropolis 1880–1930.* Toronto: Stoddard Publishing for the Canadian Centre for Architecture, 1998.

Gray, Charlotte. "First Flight," *The Beaver*, Vol. 89, No. 1 (February–March 2009), 14–22.

Griffith, Naomi. *The Contexts of Acadian History, 1686–1784.* Montreal: McGill-Queen's University Press, 1992.

Greer, Allan. *Peasant, Lord, and Merchant: Rural Society in Three Quebec Parishes 1740–1840.* Toronto: University of Toronto Press, 1985.

Greer, Carlotta C. *Foods and Home Making*. New York: Allyn and Bacon, 1928.

Harris, R. Cole, ed. *Historical Atlas of Canada, Volume I* (1987); *Volume II,* ed. R. Louis Gentilcore (1993) *et al.*; *Volume III,* ed. Donald Kerr (1990). Designer/cartographer Geoffrey J. Matthews. Toronto, Buffalo, London: University of Toronto Press.

Hayne, David M., ed. *Dictionary of Canadian Biography: Volume II*. Toronto: University of Toronto Press, 1969.

Hopkins, Anthony. *Songs from the Front & Rear: Canadian Servicemen's Songs of the Second World War*. Edmonton: Hurtig Publishers, 1979.

Housby, D, comp. *Representative Books of the Last 100 Years 1883–1983*. Toronto: Toronto Public Library, 1983.

Hughson, John W., and Courtney C.J. Bond. *Hurling Down the Pine*. Chelsea, QC: Historical Society of the Gatineau, 1964; 3rd ed. 1987.

Jack, I. Allen, Q.C., D.C.L., ed. *Biographical Review: this volume contains biographical sketches of leading citizens of the province of New Brunswick under the editorial supervision of I. Allen Jack*. Boston: Biographical Review Publishing Co., 1900.

Jarratt, Melynda. *War Brides: The Stories of the Women Who Left Everything Behind to Follow the Men They Loved*. Toronto: Dundurn Press, 2009.

Jobb, Dean. "'The first that was ever publish'd in the Province': John Bushell's *Halifax Gazette*, 1752–1761."

Royal Nova Scotia Historical Society Journal, Vol.11 (2008), 1–22.

Johnson, Steven. *The Ghost Map: The Story of London's Most Terrifying Epidemic — and How It Changed Science, Cities, and the Modern World.* New York: Riverhead Books, 2006.

Johnston, Mac. *Corvettes Canada: Convoy Veterans of WWII Tell their True Stories.* Toronto: McGraw-Hill Ryerson, 1994.

Johnstone, William D. *For Good Measure: A Complete Compendium of International Weights and Measures.* New York: Holt, Rinehart, and Winston, 1975.

Jordan, David P. *Transforming Paris: The Life and Labours of Baron Haussmann.* New York: The Free Press/Simon & Schuster, 1995.

Kay, N.W., ed. *The Practical Carpenter and Joiner, Illustrated.* London: Odhams Press Ltd., n.d.

Kennedy, Patricia. "Approaching an Iceberg: Some Guidelines for Understanding Archival Sources Relating to State Trials." *Canadian State Trials: Law, Politics, and Security Measures, 1608–1837.* F. Murray Greenwood and Barry Wright, eds. Toronto: University of Toronto Press, 1996. Appendix 1.

_____. *How To Trace Your Loyalist Ancestors.* Ottawa: Ottawa Branch OGS, 1989. Pub. No. 82–9.

_____. "The Measures of Trade," *The Archivist*, Vol. 20, No. 2 (1994), 5–8.

Kindred, Sheila. "Jane Austen's Naval Brother Charles on the North American Station 1805–1811." *Royal Nova Scotia Historical Society Journal*, Vol.10 (2007): 15–46.

_____. "James Cook: Cartographer in the Making, 1758–1762." *Royal Nova Scotia Historical Society Journal*, Vol.12 (2009), 54–81.

Kingsley, Charles. "The Three Fishers" in *Shorter Poems Revised Eidtion*. W.J. Alexander, ed. Toronto: The T. Eaton Co. Limited, 1924.

Kipling, Rudyard. "The Explorer," *Collected Verse of Rudyard Kipling*. New York: Doubleday, Page & Company, 1919.

Knowles, Elizabeth ed. *The Oxford Dictionary of Quotations Sixth Edition*. Oxford: Oxford University Press, 2004.

Laliberté, Jean-Marie, comp. *Index des greffes des notaires décédes, 1645–1948*. Quebec: B. Pontbriand, 1967.

Lamb, James B. *Corvette Navy: True Stories from Canada's Atlantic War*. Second edition. Toronto: Stoddard, 2000.

Landels, J.G. *Engineering in the Ancient World*. Berkley and Los Angeles: University of California Press, 1978.

La Tour du Pin, Henriette-Lucy Dillon de Gouvernet de. *Memoirs of Madame de La Tour du Pin*. Felice Harcourt, ed. and trans. New York: The McCall Publishing Company, 1971.

Light, Beth, and Alison Prentice, eds. *Pioneer and Gentlewomen of British North America 1713–1867*. Toronto: New Hogtown Press, 1980.

Lines, Kathleen, comp. *Lavender's Blue: A Book of Nursery Rhymes*. London: Oxford University Press, 1967.

Longley, R.S. "The Coming of the New England Planters to the Annapolis Valley." *They Planted Well*, Margaret Conrad, ed. Fredericton, NB: Acadiensis Press, 1988, 14–28.

MacLeod, Mary K. *Whisper in the Air: Marconi The Canadian Years, 1902–1946*. Hantsport, NS: Lancelot Press, 1992.

Mann, Jessica. *Out of Harm's Way: The Wartime Evacuation of Children from Britain*. London: Headline Book Publishing, 2005.

Marlatt, Michael E. "French Measurements." *The Beaver* (April–May, 1998), 46.

Masters, Roger D. *The Nature of Politics*. New Haven & London: Yale University Press, 1989.

McLean, Marianne. *The People of Glengarry: Highlanders in Transition, 1745–1820*. Montreal: McGill-Queens University Press, 1993.

Merriman, Brenda Dougall. *Genealogical Standards of Evidence: A Guide for Genealogists*. Toronto: OGS/Dundurn Press, 2010.

Mills, Elizabeth Shown. *Evidence! Citation & Analysis for the Family Historian*. Baltimore, MD: Genealogical Publishing Co., 1997.

Milne, Kim. *Children of the Country: A Guide to Indian and Métis Sources*. Winnipeg: The Manitoba Genealogical Society Inc., 1988.

Milner, Marc. *North Atlantic Run: The Royal Canadian Navy and the Battle for the Convoys*. St. Catherines, ON: Vanwell Publishing, 2006.

Morrison, James. *Aboriginal People in the Archives: A Guide to Sources in the Archives of Ontario*. Toronto: Ministry of Culture and Communication, 1982.

Nicolson, Juliet. *The Perfect Summer: Dancing into Shadow England in 1911*. London: John Murray, 2006.

Noble, Jean C. "It's A Wise Child ...," *Family Tree Magazine*. Vol.11, No.12 (Oct, 1995), 4 5.

Perez, Carlotta. *Technological Revolutions and Financial Capital, The Dynamics of Bubbles and Golden Ages*. Cheltenham, U.K.: Edward Elgar, 2002.

Pigott, Peter. *On Canadian Wings: A Century of Flight*. Toronto: Dundurn Press, 2007.

Pitcher, Dr. C. Sotheby. "A Voyage to China in 1806." *Family Tree Magazine* (August 1997), 8–10.

Pool, Daniel. *What Jane Austen Ate and Charles Dickens Knew: From Fox Hunting to Whist — the Facts of Daily Life in 19th-Century England*. New York: Temple Books, Simon & Schuster Inc., 1994.

Pound, Richard W., ed. *The Fitzhenry & Whiteside Book of Canadian Facts & Dates*. 3rd Revised Edition. Richmond Hill, ON.: Fitzhenry & Whiteside, 2003.

Pringle, Gertrude. *Etiquette in Canada: The Blue Book of Social Usage*. Toronto: McClelland & Stewart, 1932; 2nd ed. 1949.

Raddall, Thomas H. *Halifax: Warden of the North*. Toronto: McClelland & Stewart, 1948.

_____. *In My Time: A Memoir*. Toronto: McClelland & Stewart, 1977.

Raible, Chris. "'A Printer is Indispensably Necessary': The Tribulations of Canada's Earliest Printers." *The Beaver*, Vol. 77:4 (August–September 1997), 19–26.

Rhodes, Hugh. *The Bokes of Nurture of Hugh Rhodes and John Russell*. Frederick J. Furnivall, ed. London: N. Turner & Co. for the Early English Text Society, 1868.

Richardson, John. *The Local Historian's Encyclopedia*. New Barnet, Herts, England: Historical Publications Ltd., 1974; 4th revised reprint, 1983.

Rodger, N.A.M. *Naval Records for Genealogists*. London: Public Record Office, 1984.

Rogers, James Edwin Thorold. *A History of Prices and Agriculture in England, from the year after the Oxford Parliament (1259) to the commencement of the continental war (1793) compiled entirely from original and contemporaneous records*. Oxford, 1866.

Rose, George Maclean, ed. *A Cyclopedia of Canadian Biography / Representative Canadians*. Toronto: Rose Publishing Co., 1888.

Russell, Bill. *Indian Affairs Records at Library and Archives Canada: A Source for Genealogical Research*. Second edition. Toronto: Ontario Genealogical Society, 1998.

Rybczynski, Witold. *Home: A Short History of an Idea.* Markham, ON: Penguin Books Canada Ltd., 1987.

Scott-Moncrieff, David. *Veteran and Edwardian Motor Cars.* London: R.T. Batsford Ltd., 1961.

Smith, Michael J., and William P. Angley. *The McCoy Printing Company Picture Postcard Handbook 1900–1910.* London, ON: Published by the authors, 2009.

Smiles, Samuel. *The Lives of George and Robert Stephenson.* London: The Folio Society, 1975.

Snell, J.D. *Early Railways.* London: Weidenfeld and Nicholson, 1967.

Spicer, Stanley T. *Maritimers Ashore & Afloat.* Hantsport, NS: Lancelot Press, Vol. 1, 1993; Vol. 2, 1994.

Taylor, Ryan and Frances Hoffman. *Across the Waters: Ontario Immigrants' Experiences 1820–1850.* Milton, ON: Global Heritage Press, 1999.

Thomas, Gertrude I. *Food of Our Forefathers.* Philadelphia: F.A. Davis Co.; Toronto: The Ryerson Press, 1941.

Thomas, Roberta. "The Maritime History Archive, Memorial University of Newfoundland: sources for research." *Families,* Vol. 34, No. 1 (February 1995), 5–13.

Tillyard, Stella. *Aristocrats: Carolyn, Emily, Louisa and Sarah Lennox 1740–1832.* London: Chatto & Windus Ltd., 1994; Vintage, 1995.

Traill, Catherine Parr. *The Female Emigrant's Guide and Hints on Canadian Housekeeping.* (1854). Reprinted in 1855 as *The Canadian Settler's Guide*. Toronto: McClelland and Stewart, New Canadian Library, 1969.

Ulrich, Laurel Thatcher. *A Midwife's Tale: The Life of Martha Ballard, Based on Her Diary 1785–1812*. New York: Vintage Books, 1991.

Wallace, W. Stewart. *The Pedlars from Quebec and Other Papers on the Nor'Westers*. Toronto: Ryerson, 1934.

Ward, William Ernest Frank. *The Royal Navy and the Slavers: The Suppression of the Atlantic Slave Trade*. New York: Schocken Books, 1970.

Watts, Christopher T and Michael J. *My Ancestor Was a Merchant Seaman, How Can I find out More About Him?* London: The Society of Genealogists, 1986.

Williams, Glyndwr. "Family and Community in the Fur Trade." *The Beaver* (Autumn, 1983).

Wise Encyclopedia of Cookery. New York: Wm. H. Wise & Co. Inc., 1948. [no author]

Wright, Esther Clark. *The Ships of St. Martins*. Saint John: New Brunswick Museum, 1974; reprinted 1978.

"Young Ladies' Aid" of St. John's United Church. *Y.L.A. Recipes*. Moncton, NB: 1948.

Index

Other Genealogy Books

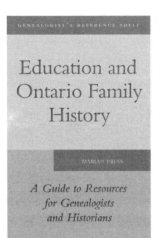

Education and Ontario Family History
A Guide to Resources for Genealogists and Historians
by Marian Press
978-1554887477
$19.99

Many family researchers with Ontario roots discover they have ancestors who were teachers. Those with no teachers in the family may have ancestors who were part of the Ontario education system as students. *Education and Ontario Family History* outlines the resources available for education from about 1785 to the early twentieth century, not only for genealogists, but also for other historians with an interest in educational records. Many historical resources are currently being digitized, and Ontario and education are no exceptions. These electronic repositories are examined in author Marian Press's book along with traditional paper and archival sources.

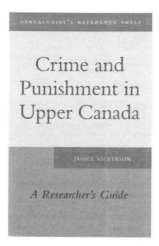

Crime and Punishment in Upper Canada
A Researcher's Guide
by Janice Nickerson
978-1554887705
$19.99

Crime and Punishment in Upper Canada provides genealogists and social historians with context and tools to understand the criminal justice system and locate sources on criminal activity and its consequences for the Upper Canada period (1791–1841) of Ontario's history. Illustrative examples further aid researchers in this era of the province's past, which is notoriously difficult to investigate due to paucity of records and indexes. An entertaining, educational read, the book features chapters with detailed inventories of available records in federal, provincial, and local repositories; published transcripts and indexes; online transcripts and indices; and suggestions for additional reading.

A Better Place
Death and Burial in
Nineteenth-Century Ontario
by Susan Smart
978-1554888993
$19.00

A Better Place describes the practices around death and burial in nineteenth-century Ontario. The book describes the pioneer funeral in detail as well as the factors that changed this simple funeral into the elaborate etiquette-driven Victorian funeral at the end of the century. It includes the sources of various funeral customs, including the origins of embalming that gave rise to the modern-day funeral parlour. The evolution of cemeteries is explained with the beginnings of cemeteries in specific towns given as examples.

DUNDURN PRESS
www.dundurn.com

What did you think of this book?
Visit www.dundurn.com
for reviews, videos, updates, and more!